The Muslim Marriage Guide

The Muslim Marriage Guide

Ruqayyah Waris Maqsood

amana publications

© Ruqayyah Waris Maqsood 1995, 1999
First published 1995 by
The Quilliam Press Ltd.,
80 Lamble Street,
London NW5 4AB

Reprinted 1999

US edition published 2000 by
amana publications
10710 Tucker Street
Beltsville, Maryland 20705-2223 USA
Tel: (301) 595-5777 Fax: (301) 595-5888
Email: amana@igprinting.com • Website: amana-publications.com

Library of Congress Cataloging-in-Publication Data

Maqsood, Ruqaiyyah Waris.
   The Muslim marriage guide / Ruqayyah Waris Maqsood.
      p. cm.
   Originally published: London : Quilliam Press, 1995.
   Includes bibliographical references.
   ISBN 0-915957-99-X
   1. Marriage--Religious aspects--Islam. 2. Family--Koranic teaching.
I. Title.
   HQ525.I8 M35 2000
   297.5'77--dc21

                                                                    00-064371

I will lie down with my love
upon this bed of petals.
If there are thorns
I will not feel them;
or if I feel them,
I will not show that
I feel them
                                        R.W.M.

Printed in the United States by
International Graphics
Beltsville, Maryland 20705-2223 USA
Tel: (301) 595-5999 • Fax: (301) 595-5888
Email: ig@igprinting.com • Website: www.igprinting.com

Contents

1 *Getting Married*

'And We have created everything in pairs, that perhaps you may remember.' (Quran, 51:49)

So you are getting married? Congratulations, and may God bless you and bring you and your chosen partner to a long and happy life together!

Leaving your childhood behind, and becoming man and wife together, is the most important step short of actually becoming Muslim that any human being can take in the interests of their own happiness and wellbeing.

'And among Allah's signs is this: that He created for you spouses from among yourselves, so that you might find rest in them; and He has set between you love and compassion. Truly there are signs in this for people who reflect.' (Quran, 20:21)

'Our Lord, grant us the delight of our eyes from our wives and our offspring ... ' (Quran, 25:74)

Marriage is such an important step that our Blessed Prophet (ﷺ) spoke of marriage as being 'half the religion': 'Whoever has married has completed half of his religion; therefore let him fear Allah in the other half!' (Bayhaqi)

You have only to use your eyes and your ears, and consider the marriages of those people you know in your own circle of family, friends and acquaintances, to know that this is so.

If your marriage is happy and fulfilled, then no matter what troubles may beset you, no matter what hardships you are obliged to face as you pass along your road of life, no matter what sicknesses or distressing circumstances, you will always face them as if your back were against a protecting fortress, inside the walls of which you may set aside all the terrors and traumas for a while, and be loved.

But marriage is also a most demanding training-ground of faith. By claiming it to be 'half the religion' the Blessed Prophet was not making an idle statement. When a human couple strive hard to get their marriage and family right in the eyes of God, they are indeed well on the road to Paradise.

For it is love which makes a marriage - not a soppy, sentimental kind of romantic dream, but the sort of love which will roll up its sleeves and get stuck into the mess; the sort of love which will hang on to you when everyone else has turned against you and is speaking wrongly of you, while you have confidence that your partner (who knows you better than any person) will justify that confidence, and spring to your defence.

Sounds too good to be true? Those of you who have grown up in unhappy circumstances, in families shaken by frustrations and depressions, where the adults were bitter and cynical, and over-authoritarian, may well wonder if it is possible to have such a loving relationship with another human being.

By the grace of God, it *is* possible, and it is what Allah intended for you, by the practice of Islam which is submission to His compassionate will.

But a happy marriage is not simply 'made in Heaven'. It does not just happen by accident.

You could go into a most beautiful garden and be amazed at the profusion and lushness of the flowers, the neatness of the borders and grasses, the absence of marauding insects and pests - and you would never for a moment think that this had come about by accident. You would know, straight away, that the garden had been created by a person or team of people who *loved* gardening, and no matter what the setbacks and problems were determined to produce a thing of great beauty and joy. A marriage is cultivated in exactly the same way.

You have to be able to see in your mind's eye the sort of garden/ marriage you would like to have when it is finished, and aim towards it. If events turn out slightly differently to what you

8

expected, it does not matter all that much, because your master-plan will be there to keep you heading in the right direction, and all unexpected events will simply be incorporated into moving to-wards this plan.

Carrying on with the garden imagery, you have to be able to recognise the seeds that you are planting, and weed out the plants you don't want before they cause trouble. Some seeds develop into beautiful flowers, while others are troublesome weeds - like bind-weed, which climbs over everything else and chokes it, until the garden is buried and destroyed.

You have to be on the alert for invasions of malicious pests which, although they are themselves claiming a right to live, are nevertheless gaining their living at the expense of yours, and are ruining the things you have planted.

You have to keep an eye on the weather, and when there is not enough rainfall, you must do the long chore of going round the garden yourself carrying water, making sure everything is all right. In a long, dry spell, this might mean a great deal of drudgery - but you know that without it your garden will fail and die. It is up to you to keep everything going.

All devout Muslims, men and women, should remember this fact, in case they think that in marriage God has granted them something in which they can just lounge about and 'watch the flowers grow'. God never grants human beings this privilege. Whatever they have that gives them pleasure, they have to work for it - they really have to earn the right to be its steward.

Everything in life is a gift, and does not belong as of right to any person. Even your body is a gift, enjoyed (or not enjoyed!) by your soul for the duration of its sojourn on earth. It is not there as a permanent feature of the universe; in fact, there are *no* permanent features of the universe - not even the rocks from which the great mountains are formed!

God has made us stewards, the *khulafa*; the guardians of this wondrous planet and its life-forms. And the most important life-form that we will ever have to cherish is our own partner, our husband or wife. From that person, we are intended to produce in love the Muslims of the next generation, and set them on their own ways with our examples and encouragement. With that person, we are supposed to build up our own lives, free from fears and resentments and uncertainties, so that we can concentrate on filling our 'space' with love and the service of God.

This is why marriage is 'half the religion'. Islam is intended to cover every aspect of a believer's life, twenty-four hours per day. Our relationship with our life-partner and family certainly accounts for at least half of this time, and for some women, it occupies one hundred percent of their time.

We neglect this most vital charge laid upon us at our peril. No human being was intended to live in isolation- either splendid isolation, thinking himself or herself 'better' than the common herd in any way, or in grief-stricken isolation, deprived of life's comforts and the satisfying of natural appetites and needs. God created Man and Woman from a single soul, and He intended them to live and work together.

'O humanity; fear your Lord, Who created you from a single soul, and from it created its spouse, and from the two of them did spread forth a multitude of men and women.' (4:1)

'We created you from a single pair of male and female'. (49:13; see also 35:11)

In this is a sure sign. Each is necessary to the other. People may live and work and have faith on their own, but it is only a 'half-life'.

As any single person, or widow living alone, or abandoned half of a couple will tell you, it is *possible* to survive and live by yourself, and even to wring some enjoyment out of this life - for you are free to be selfish and do the things you want to do without much consideration of the needs and wants of others. But there is a terrible price for this solitary existence.

It is like a blind person developing extra-sensitive hearing in order to compensate and cope with lack of sight; or a paralysed person in a wheelchair developing extra-large arm muscles to make up for the lack of legs. It can be done - but it is a miserable and long process.

Married life brings its pressures, but it can also provide the kind of relaxation that human beings naturally need. Imam al-Ghazali observes that:

> 'One of the benefits of marriage is the enjoyment of the company and the sight of one's spouse, and by shared amusement, whereby the heart is refreshed and strengthened for worship; for the soul is prone to boredom and is inclined to shun duty as something

unnatural to it. If forced to persevere in something it dislikes, it shies and backs away, whereas if it is revived from time to time by pleasures it acquires new strength and vigour.'
(*Ihya Ulum al-Din*)

The sign and the design that God intended is that it is best for men and women to come together as a team.

People work together as all sorts of teams - they cooperate for the sake of games and sport; they unite to do a task too great for an individual, like building a house; they sort themselves out into managers and workers in order to create businesses and earn a living. But the most fundamental team of all, and the one which is the most important, is that of a man and woman deciding to live together in one space as husband and wife.

2 *The Key to a Happy Marriage*

'Actions are only (judgèd) by intentions; each person shall be rewarded only for that which he intended.'

(Bukhari and Muslim)

All human beings share the same basic needs - to feel needed, to be appreciated, respected and loved. Without these needs, a human being cannot really be said to be human. And the most obvious thing about these needs is that they all depend absolutely on the relationship of one person with another.

So basic are they that one can surely take evidence from them that the need for people to find partners, and mate, and interact together with each other and then in the creation of happy, stable families, is intended by our Creator as a sign.

The family is the oldest of all human institutions, and entire civilisations have flourished or disappeared depending on whether family life was strong or weak. Yet all over the world today, and not just in the West, families are breaking down and societies are disintegrating into confusion and despair. Hence the central importance which Islam attaches to family values, and to the art - and it is an art - of making this most basic of all relationships work.

Embarking on a marriage is really very similar to beginning the construction of a building. The building may be extremely magificent and grand, but the most important thing about it is the foundations upon which it is built. If those foundations are not secure, the building will not survive when the storms and shocks of

12

stress hit it, as they inevitably will sooner or later.

What does a husband need to do in order to gain his wife's respect? And why does it matter so much to him? And why does a woman have such a powerful need for a husband's love? How can she earn it, and keep him faithful to her? Our Lord has revealed guidelines for human life together since the dawn of time, and for over fourteen centuries Muslims have had the example of the life of the Prophet Muhammad (ﷺ). Wise counsel on how to build the foundations of a marriage, and then to create a happy family, have been freely available for anyone to consult. Muslims believe that whether people follow these guidelines or not actually determines not only their earthly happiness, but also their eternal fate once their earthly life is finished.

There are really two keys to a happy marriage. The first is to love Allah, and to seek to apply His principles in every situation and relationship. The second is to do a little sensible soul-searching and analysis before embarking on such an important enterprise - one that is going to be the most profound commitment in the whole of your life, and is going to affect the lives and wellbeing of so many people, not only your own!

What does a person want from marriage? Before committing themselves to a life-partner, every individual should try to sit down calmly and become conscious of what their needs really are, and consider whether or not the proposed partner is going to prove likely to be able to fulfil those needs. These needs are not just for a man to have a cheap servant or concubine (a maid, or an available sex-partner for whenever he feels 'in the mood'); or for a woman to have someone to shower her with gifts, clothes, jewellery and flowers, or to provide the means for her to cradle in her arms a beloved baby (a sugar-daddy or a stud-bull). The needs amount to much more than that. They are physical, emotional, and also spiritual.

What are your values and your goals, and how do you expect to achieve them? You have to know yourself pretty well, and also have a fair idea of whether or not your intended spouse under-stands them and is willing and able to satisfy them.

Furthermore, if your marriage is to be successful, you must also be considerate towards the legitimate needs of your partner, and not just look to your own gratification. If you are going to be happy, then your spouse must be happy also, or your relationship is doomed.

We have physical needs, not only for sexual satisfaction but also for food, clothing and shelter.

We also have emotional needs - for understanding, kindness and compassion. We have the need for companionship and friendship, a person with whom we can share our intimate thoughts and still feel secure; someone who we know is not going to laugh at us or mock us, but is going to care about us. We need to feel that we are building something up together, and accomplishing something that is good.

Then, we have the spiritual need for inner peace and contentment. We need to feel at home with a partner whose way of life is compatible with our own sense of morality, and our desire to live in such a way as is pleasing to God. If our religion means anything at all to us, then the most fundamental need we have is to find someone whose Islam is not just on the lips, but has reached the heart.

We will not feel comfortable if we are settled in a life partnership with someone whose ways, morals or habits make us uneasy or disapproving - that would not make for our inner peace, but would be a terrible worry. We want to feel secure. This has nothing to do with satisfying our urges for career, fame, wealth, and material possessions. Such things are pleasant enough, but Muslims know that there is a hunger of the spirit that remains even after all these physical needs are satisfied. The love of *dunya* - the things of this world - is a tricky illusion. Muslims know that no matter how pleasant they may be, the things of this world are ephemeral and will pass away quickly: they are dependent on the will of Allah. A millionaire can be ground into the dust at the slightest turn of fate. Nothing of the earth's riches can be taken with us when we leave here to make the journey that comes after this brief life in the world.

Our spirits long to know who we are, what we are, why we are here, where we are going, and how we can get there. Non-believers scoff at religion, but find their hearts are not at ease because they do not have the answers to these questions. Muslims feel that even if they do not know all the details for certain, at least they are on the right road. Even if they do not always know the reason why Allah has given a particular instruction, they trust His judgement, and

14

know it is right to carry it out, and that in doing so they will find happiness and contentment.

So, when we are about to embark upon marriage, we need to be aware of how we feel about all these issues - and also, how our chosen partner feels. Of course, it is impossible to sit down and thrash out all the answers in five minutes. The greatest brains in the world spend whole lifetimes on these issues. Nevertheless, it is sensible to at least be aware of the issues - even if we cannot come up with all the answers - and to have talked about them frankly to the intended spouse.

To make a successful marriage, it is also vital that you take into consideration the needs and nature of your partner. What he or she believes about 'life, the universe and everything' is important in the pursuit of your own happiness and success. For if only one half of the partnership is happy and fulfilled by the relationship, it will not be long before both are affected.

People intending to marry need to know from the outset whether or not they are *compatible* with each other. This means more than whether or not they are from a suitable family, or whether they are practicing the basic obligations of the faith: such things are important, but to believe that they are all that matters may lead to disaster. Sometimes, when one has fallen in love one is almost in a state of sickness which impairs the mental state. They say 'love is blind': as Imam Busiri says in his poem *Al-Burda*: 'You have besieged me with advice, but I hear it not; For the man in love is deaf to all reproaches.' Often the person in love is so besotted with the beloved that they simply cannot see the things that are 'wrong' with the loved one. Or if they can, they assume that their love is so powerful that it will overcome all obstacles and incompatibilities, and will be able to influence the beloved to change according to the desires and tastes of the lover.

Some hope! If two people are not well-suited as a team, then the going is likely to be rough. According to an old Middle Eastern proverb, a field cannot be properly ploughed if an ox and a donkey are yoked together. Such a performance might be possible, but it would cause pain and hardship to both.

The same applies in marriage. If a man and woman have totally different interests, tastes, pastimes, and types of friends, it is a dead cert that their marriage will soon come under strain. This is one

15

good reason why it is important for life-partners to have a shared attitude to their religion. Allah has prohibited marriage to polytheists, and has commanded us to marry people of religion. He has also approved the involvement of parents and guardians in the choice of spouse.

Family backgrounds often have a great deal to do with the set of values people have. When the backgrounds of both husband and wife are similar, they will probably find it easier to grow together. However, Allah and His Prophet (ﷺ) have stated that people from widely different backgrounds can make very good marriages, so long as their attitude to their religion is compatible.

> 'A slave who believes is better (for you) than an idolatress, though she attract you.' (Quran, 2:221)

> 'A woman is married for four reasons: for her property, her rank, her beauty and her religion. Win the one who is religious, and you will prosper.' (Bukhari and Muslim)

Many marriages these days end up in unhappiness or even divorce on the grounds of incompatibility. If the partners had stood aside from the issue of 'being in love' for a moment, and had been careful to examine their actual compatibility instead, these tragedies might have been averted. Hence the importance of intelligent parental help in selecting and assessing potential partners!

Sincere respect for each other is the most vital element - not so-called 'closeness' and physical intimacy before marriage. Unbridled passion might seem flattering at first, but it actually betrays a selfish unconcern for the other person's happiness. It might also sow seeds of doubt that could later give rise to uncertainty as to the real motive for the marriage. Was it merely to provide an outlet for passion, or was it genuinely to share a lifetime with someone who is truly appreciated and loved? *Many find out to their cost that lack of self-control before marriage frequently foreshadows lack of self-control afterwards.*

However, it is never possible for two people to be completely compatible in every respect, for they are two separate individuals, each with a distinct soul and personality. If one partner simply tries to dominate the other so as to wipe out the other spouse's person-

16

ality, tragedy is on the way. One of the biggest dangers of 'macho' males is that after a very short period of married life they tend to think of their partners in terms of 'wife' or 'extension of self', or even 'property', and forget that Islam recognises women as persons in their own right.

When husbands on the brink of divorce are interviewed by counsellors such as the Relate teams, they frequently realise with a shock that even though they might have been married for years and have perhaps expected their wives to pander to their every whim, they do not have the least idea what their wife's favourite colour, or dress, or hobby is, or who their friends are. They simply never noticed any aspect of their wife that did not specifically relate to *them*.

People are not perfect, of course; we all have shortcomings. A spouse might not be aware of the shortcomings of his or her partner before marriage, but will certainly pick up this awareness pretty soon afterwards. Some marriages virtually die in the honeymoon period, if some awful, unsuspected habit is suddenly revealed in the intimacy of the bedroom. A friend of mine, for example, accepted her arranged marriage quite happily, until she discovered that her new husband had disgusting personal habits, and even threw his meal leftovers out of the window! It proved impossible to cure these shortcomings, so the marriage was swiftly doomed.

So, if you love him, but you are irritated by the way he always leaves a mess for others to clear up, never gives you a little gift or remembers important dates, and you find the way he picks his nose or honks out his throat disgusting, he is going to drive you crazy after marriage. And if you adore her, but you wish she didn't witter on quite so much, or talk about you to her friends, or go into sulks and tears at the slightest thing, or cling to you quite so tightly when you are going out - then the gazing at you and talking at you will soon pall, and you'll be off with your friends to get a break from it, only to return later to the tantrums and the tears.

If you can see his or her faults, and love him or her anyway (without changes), and are able to live with your irritation - fair enough. But if you know that would be impossible, think twice. Suppose your pet hate was dirty socks, but your man wears them until they stick to the wall if thrown there? I knew such a man. Over

17

twenty years of nagging had no effect on him. Suppose the smell of pipe smoke makes you feel sick? Yes, he may say he'll give it all up for you - but we've all met failed non-smokers before!

It is not the shortcomings themselves that make a marriage fail, but the inability to communicate about them, and tackle them, or make allowances for them. Are you flexible enough to make allowances, as you wish allowances to be made for you? Do the good points of your loved one outweigh the bad? Love certainly does cover a multitude of sins; but do you really love *that* person enough, or were you really only in love with a dream of what you would like your loved one to be, and not the real person, warts and all?

Some men and women never give up their 'dream lovers', ideals created in their own fantasies. They spend a lifetime hankering after that ideal, or trying to mould the one they have into that ideal. By 'mould', we occasionally mean 'force'. Either way, it is pretty miserable and insulting for the one whose natural character is being rejected.

Sometimes people are 'in love with love', and crave the excitement and satisfaction of continual romance. Once the more down-to-earth partner begins to settle in, they feel taken for granted and starved of affection, and the craving for the fire of fresh love overcomes the domestic cosiness and contentment, which seems so dull by comparison. Their ideal lover would present his or her soul on a plate to them every time they gaze into each other's eyes. They never realise that the dream person does not exist beyond their own fantasies. Consequently, they are always in the 'pain' of love, dissatisfied, frustrated lovers, and do not make good marriage material. In Muslim marriage, it is reality that counts.

It is foolish not to think seriously about the problems that other people can see, and ignore the wise advice of those who care about you. Those who simply close their eyes and minds to unpleasant details before marriage will certainly have to face them later, when the need to be on best behaviour has gone and both partners are reverting to type. It is vitally important for husband and wife to see the other person as he or she really is, and also to be honest in presenting their true selves to their partners. Marriages based on fantasy, fakery and illusion are doomed.

3 *What is a Good Muslim Marriage Like?*

'You shall not enter Paradise until you have faith, and you shall not have faith until you love one another. Have compassion on those who are on earth, and He Who is in Heaven will have compassion for you.'

(Hadith in Bukhari)

Firstly, a good Muslim marriage should show *welcome*. Even if the wife did not spend all her day in the home, but perhaps had some employment outside it - even so, the Muslim home should be ready to welcome the family and the guest.

It is the most miserable thing in the world to come home to a dark, locked house, totally empty and bereft of human presence - and this is particularly crushing to a new husband or a child. Any wife thinking of taking up some kind of employment should bear this in mind. Where children are involved, she should make some arrangement with a relative or helper so that they do not build up a mental picture of a home where they 'don't count', where they do not feel welcome. As regards a husband, as he is an adult he should not ignore the problems, but be able to talk the thing through and see what the difficulties are, and be able to support the best possible solution that is acceptable to them both.

In an Islamic marriage, both husband and wife have responsibilities and duties, and both are individuals responsible before God for their own Records. Neither has the right to impose or force the

19

other to do something against religion, or to make the other suffer.

It is no good, of course, the husband simply feeling 'hard done-by' if he wishes to accept the wife's earnings as part of the total income of the household, but then makes a fuss if it is he who returns to the house first, and who might, perhaps, be expected in that case to light the oven or make the tea! Obviously, if the wife returns before the husband, it is she who gets the 'dark emptiness', and she is naturally expected to accept this as part of the way things are. To some extent, it is not really 'part of the way things are' any more, in a society where the women are increasingly joining the men as part of the country's workforce. This has to be acknowledged.

The correct Islamic attitude should always be to seek out the *best* way, and not insist on any code of conduct that is going to upset either partner, or make either partner suffer unfairly. It means that sometimes a husband may have to take the rough with the smooth, or it may mean that the wife may find it better for her marriage not to take full-time employment, if this threatens to put too much strain on the marriage. Everything should be considered fairly and openly.

It is patently *not* all right to expect a highly intelligent woman to sit around at home wasting her life's talents by limiting herself to housework alone. It is true that there is serious unemployment in many Muslim societies, and a major influx of women into the jobs market would make this much worse and leave many families without one breadwinner, let alone two. But it is also true that the Muslim world is crying out for female doctors, nurses, lecturers and so forth, and these women have to undergo considerable sacrifice in order to get themselves trained, and expect to be able to offer their services to the community in much the same way as a trained man. It is *not* the duty of a Muslim man to be selfish and deprive the community of these talented and dedicated women, and expect them to limit themselves to the service of just one man. So many men take the talents of their wives for granted, and stultify their possible development, which is such a great pity, and a tragedy for society.

On another level, there are many women who cannot cope with being confined all day with children and domestic affairs, who long to go out to work simply to have something else to do, other people to see and talk to, and a little financial reward at the end of it. A Muslim man should realise that he is a lucky person indeed if his wife is happy to devote her whole time and attention to him and his needs, and those of their children and relations. He should count his blessings and never forget to appreciate what a treasure he has been granted.

In many Muslim societies it is taken for granted that a married woman will pass her life in this way, and only someone who has travelled extensively from Muslim country to Muslim country, and had access and the ability to observe the life of Muslim women, can comment fairly on the enormous weight of boredom that lies over the lives of many of these sisters.

It is not full Islam - for God would not have given women the ability to be professionally employed if He had intended a wholly different vocation for them. The Prophet's (⬥) first wife Khadija was first his employer, while his cousin-wife Zaynab continued to work after their marriage. She made and sold excellent leather saddles, and the Prophet (⬥) was very pleased with her work. When Islam began fourteen hundred years ago, the women around the Prophet participated in public life, were vocal about social inequalities, and often shared decision-making with him. This continued through the the golden age of Muslim civilization, when women occupied a far more central role in society than they do nowadays. There were colleges like Cairo's Saqlatuniya Academy which provided higher education for women, and were staffed by women professors. The biographical dictionaries of the great hadith scholars reveal that about a sixth of the hadith scholars in the Muslim middle ages were women. Historians today also marvel at the major role which Muslim women played in the medieval economy, a role made possible by the fact that Islamic law grants a woman the right to own and dispose of property independently of her husband, a law only introduced in the West at the beginning of the twentieth century! But it cannot be denied that over the past three hundred years of our history, women have increasingly disappeared from such positions. It is our duty to try and revive the classical Muslim tradition in this important area.

All this reminds us that true submission to God in Islam means that each individual must do the very best possible to make use of all their talents and abilities, for the greater good of the community.

21

If the person involved happens to be a Muslim woman, there is the extra responsibility that the household and family must not suffer, and the onus really falls on her. Any Muslim woman worth her salt will work out a satisfactory way of fulfilling all her obligations, and any Muslim man bearing this in mind should be supportive and sympathetic, and willing to pitch in and give practical help when required.

The *sunna* of the Blessed Prophet in this respect was revealed by his wife A'isha. A hadith in Bukhari tells us that when asked what he did at home, she replied that he helped his wives with their work until it was time to go out to lead the prayers. As a perfect gentleman and the leader of the Muslim nation, he did not regard helping his wives as a slur on his manhood.

If the wife spends all her time caring for her home, then her man must appreciate this sacrifice and devote sufficient time to her as reward for her efforts. He should notice what she has done, and take an interest in it. It is not good Islam simply to take everything for granted, and insult the wife's stalwart efforts by regarding them simply as a man's right. A good Muslim husband will obviously not distress his wife by going off boozing and flirting with other women, but neither should he just pop into the house for a meal and then rush off out again with his male friends and spend excessive hours in their company (even at the mosque), leaving the wife alone in the evening when she might have hoped to share a little of his time.

It is a commonplace 'blindness' in many societies that only the employed people are 'working', and the ones at home are not. True Muslims should never forget that the money brought in for the family's support is earned by a joint effort; if husbands think they are the sole earners and breadwinners, then they should stop to figure out what it would cost them if they lost their wives and were obliged to hire a purchasing agent, a cook, a kitchen-hand, a cleaner, a housekeeper, a decorator, a nursemaid, a chauffeur for the children, and so on. Normally the wife saves all this expense by doing this work herself - quite a contribution!

If the wife does go out to work, then extra thought and organisation are obviously needed, if the home is not to lose out. This might mean that a husband would be expected to do more in the way of housework than he might really want to do - and in fairness, if a woman is working long hours as well as the man, then he is a poor Muslim if he does not do his fair share around the house.

Some Muslim men need reminding that the various fatwas (authoritative pronouncements in religious law) on who has responsibility for housework actually vary quite a lot from *madhhab* to *madhhab*, and that there is no fixed and rigid Islamic ruling in this respect. The Hanafis, for example (who include most Muslims in Britain), regard housework as a religious obligation binding upon the wife. Yet the position of the classical Shafi'i school is quite different:

> 'A woman is not obliged to serve her husband by baking, grinding flour, cooking, washing, or any other kind of service, because the marriage contract entails, for her part, only that she let him enjoy her sexually, and she is not obliged to do other than that.'
> (*Reliance of the Traveller*, tr. Keller, p.948.)

If the man is not prepared or able to do his fair share, then other things have to be done when a woman goes out to work: cleaners, gardeners and baby-minders have to be hired to help. With good organisation, it can be done. A Muslim wife who let her home go to ruin while she made money outside would be at fault; but the responsibility of seeing that all runs smoothly is up to both husband and wife. There is no point whatsoever in a wife collapsing with exhaustion to the disgust of an unsympathetic husband. The Islamic way is one of love and consideration, and unselfish sharing.

Another aspect of welcome is in the generous reception of guests, which is regarded as an important Islamic duty. In Islam, the guest needs no invitation, even to come and stay for a few days, though it is obviously good manners if the visitor can inform the host in advance of his or her arrival. When guests come, Muslims should be hospitable and generous, whether or not they expect to get the same treatment in return.

As regards the guest, you do not know whom God will send you, or for what reason - therefore you should always be prepared, no matter how humble the guest, or how inconvenient - and your household should always be welcoming. To achieve this, it has to be well ordered, with thoughtful and considerate catering.

A guest cannot be welcomed if the cupboards are bare, and the furniture is dirty or broken-down, or if the husband and wife are seething with anger and resentment for each other.

To this end, it is very important that Muslim men learn properly the principles of Islam when considering both the guest and the person who caters for the guest - who is, of course, usually the wife. It is bad manners to bring back people unexpectedly, unless this really cannot be helped, especially in a society that has full use of the telephone! Even then, a good guest should not expect to be entertained lavishly if no warning has been given - for the cupboard could be bare, or the wife could be sick or exhausted, or vitally engaged in some other planned activity. It is one thing to welcome the guest as the 'gift of Allah', but it is quite another thing for people to impose rudely on others without thought for their convenience. If this happens, the wife can at least console herself with the thought that her sacrifice and good manners will be recorded to her benefit, whereas the guest's and the husband's rudeness will have to be accounted for!

Allah has taught that although a good wife will always be hospitable, a Muslim should not enter another's house before seeking permission (sura 24:27-8), even from those very close to him or her - for people in their homes may be in a state of dress or mood in which they do not wish to be seen. The Prophet (ﷺ) said that if a man arrived home earlier than expected he should wait, so that 'the woman who has not dressed may have time to smarten herself, and one whose husband was away might take a bath and become neat and clean.' (Bukhari)

The Prophet (ﷺ) taught that it was wrong to bang loudly on a door, for someone might be asleep or ill inside the house. Furthermore, unexpected callers should not persist if they suspect the householders do not wish to answer them. If there is no response after knocking (or ringing) three times, the Prophet (ﷺ) instructed that the caller should tactfully leave.

The Prophet (ﷺ) was exceedingly generous, and encouraged Muslims to be similarly generous to guests, letting them stay overnight if need be - but he limited this automatic right of hospitality to three days. The principle is that no guest should stay so long as to become a nuisance or a burden. He said:

A Good Muslim Marriage

'The entertainment of a guest is three days, but unstinting kindness and courtesy is for a day and a night. It is not permitted for
a Muslim to stay with his brother until he makes him sinful.' They
said: 'O Messenger of God! How would he make him sinful?' He
replied: 'By staying with him so long that no provisions are left
with which to entertain him.'

In normal circumstances, a good Muslim wife should never be
totally unprepared, or caught without something to offer as hospitality. At the least, the guest should be able to expect 'pot luck', a
simple drink and cake or biscuit; but should then go and not linger
excessively. The Sunna of the Prophet makes it quite clear that he
always advised giving proper warning when a guest was coming,
so that the wife could have things ready, and not be shamed by the
thoughtlessness of her husband.

The second quality needed in a Muslim home is *commitment*.
This means commitment from both partners, of course. It must be
obvious even to newlyweds that people cannot go through life
without annoying each other, irritating each other, letting each
other down in all sorts of ways, and making mistakes. Commitment means that when things start to go wrong, neither partner will
give up and run away.

In many parts of the world marriages are quickly broken because
the partners take the view that if it doesn't work out, then they'll
end it. They regard their marriages as *conditional*. Where that
viewpoint exists, the marriage is almost doomed from the start, and
generally produces pain and heartache.

Threatening to walk out is a kind of blackmail that can have dire
consequences. It brings insecurity, making the partner who is to be
left behind convinced that the other does not really love them. It
puts the nasty sneak-feeling of being abandoned in the back of the
listener's mind. It is especially dangerous to make this kind of
threat if 'walking out' means abandoning someone who cannot
cope on their own, or returning to a foreign country.

Once two people have committed themselves to each other, they
should move mountains in order to stay together, rather than let
silly things come between them. A good rule is never to go to bed
in anger with a quarrel unresolved. Sometimes proud people find
it incredibly difficult to make 'peace terms' with each other when
they have fallen out; in a good marriage some kind of code or

signalling is sometimes an enormous help. You do not feel like falling at the feet of your spouse in abject apology, but you do not wish to prolong hostilities. A pet word, or phrase or gesture is what is needed as a kind of 'white flag'; when it is recognised, it gives a chance to cool down and restore good humour. My own husband (fresh from Pakistan) and I used to have blazing rows over all sorts of things which often got quite frightening for me; but I always knew when the 'rough wind' was blowing over when he grunted that I was a 'bloody Englishwoman'! It was hardly a compliment, but it was my little signal that peace was on its way, and sure enough, our arms were around each other before very long - even if neither side refused to give in!

The third vital quality is *sense of humour*, something our Blessed Prophet (ﷺ) understood very well. No marriage will survive without it. The ability to see the funny side of things has saved sanity and avoided bloodshed in many a tricky situation. One of the lovely things about a successful marriage is that when the storm clouds have blown over, one can often look back and laugh at whatever it was that had seemed such a serious and vital matter at the time. A sense of humour helps a person to keep things in perspective.

It helps one to cope when your mother-in-law is breathing heavily down your neck, or when some eminent visitor has called unexpectedly and caught you at your worst; it helps you to cope with that apparent law of nature (actually a trial) that if it is possible for a thing to go wrong or get worse it will choose the most inconvenient (and public) moment to do so.

It helps you to look objectively at what went wrong, and put your failing into perspective; most of our human failings are pretty common, and shared by the vast majority of humanity. Sometimes things that seemed so serious to us at the time when they happened become just a story to be told with a laugh when you recount them later to others.

The fourth quality is *patience*, which goes hand-in-hand with *tolerance* and *consideration*. A Muslim learns to be patient in so many ways. In the early days and weeks of marriage, young couples are often impatient to have all the things that they were used to in their parents' homes - but this is obviously unreasonable, unless you are very wealthy. Sometimes it took your parents a lifetime to collect up all their worldly bits and pieces. You are only just beginning, and you cannot have everything in the first five minutes.

Sometimes the new husband complains that his wife can't cook like his mother. But how does he know how well his mother could cook when *she* first got married? It may be that his wife is actually doing better than she did!

Sometimes a new wife complains that her husband isn't bringing in the money like her father used to. But how does she know how her father struggled when he first got married?

If you are given everything without having to work for it, you will not value it and be thankful for it. Nobody would. It is important for your relationship that you grow together, and work together, and build up your home with its own particular atmosphere, together.

There are two serious dangers here - a 'martyrdom' complex (the one doing all the work and making all the sacrifices and/or decisions), and a 'not-my-home' complex (the one who is left out, or who chooses not to get involved). If only one of you does all the work or all the planning, the other partner will never feel that he or she fully belongs, and may even become resentful - which seems so strange to the partner who has done all the donkey work 'for' the other. Build your home together, so that its atmosphere is created by both of you, then neither side will be resentful or undervalue the sacrifice of the other.

You are no longer a single person, but have a companion to share your life with. It takes time and effort to blend two lives together in harmony. Many romantic stories end when the couple get married and they live 'happily ever after'. In real life, the wedding is just the first chapter, and it is the living happily afterwards, day by day, that presents the challenge. There is not a lot of thrill in getting up early, going to work, doing the chores, and so on.

Like a lot of people nowadays, you may have launched your marriage with expectations that were not very realistic; and when these were not met, you came down with a big dose of disappointment and dismay. Yes, it can come as a shock when you are no longer living alone (when you can do as you like), or with a family that you have been with all your life and are used to. You might suddenly discover that you don't know the new person you are with as well as you thought you did. The success of your marriage

27

and your happiness will depend upon your willingness to make allowances, and adjust.

Be *tolerant* with the other person's ways, likes and dislikes. Give the other person room. So many marriages are spoiled by wives or husbands clinging desperately on to their spouse, unwilling to let them do the least little thing on their own. This can be a terrible mistake, for no matter how much you may love that other person, you cannot change him or her into *you*. There will be all sorts of things that your partner would like to do, which he or she may not feel they can do once they get married. This is a great pity, and brings loss into the relationship rather than gain.

Try to organise your life together so that you do have some space that is your own, and some activities which are your own too. This could become of vital importance if the husband is one of those Muslims who starts spending more and more time away on that most innocent of pleasures - his time at the mosque. Two things are important - firstly, that the wife can accept cheerfully that he *does* want to go, and that it is good for him to do so; and secondly that the husband does not make his trips out to the mosque an excuse to neglect his wife and family.

The teaching of the Blessed Prophet was quite clear on this score - a man who neglected his wife was not the 'best of Muslims' and was *not* scoring 'good points' for himself by his long hours away from her and his family - even if he was busily saying extra voluntary prayers. Such prayers can be said at home. It is real neglect if he is still behaving like a single man, and is just socialising with his male friends! Once again, a really abandoned wife might find consolation in the realisation that she will be earning merit for coping with this distressing situation. He, of course, will be building up sins of omission for which he will one day be called to account.

Try not to nag. This only gives the nagged partner an extra excuse to stay away - to avoid the nagging! The Prophet Suleiman (﷽) once said 'a nagging wife is like water endlessly dripping.'

Women are often more emotional than men, and more inclined to give vent to their feelings when they are upset about something, and they may also feel that this is the only weapon they have. But this kind of emotional pressure only alienates husbands, it does not solve the problem. It is simply a wife's duty as a Muslima to point out both sides of the situation, and leave her partner to draw his own conclusions, and take the responsibility for his own action, or lack of it.

Think, and be compassionate, before you criticise. Before a wife wonders where her romantic suitor has vanished to, now that her husband takes her for granted, she should try to understand that he may be stressed and working hard in today's demanding workplace to be a good provider, and struggling with his new responsibilities. Likewise, before a husband wonders what has happened to the glamorous young lady he married, who has 'changed, now that she has got her man', notice whether she is working hard to cook and clean, and gets tired and does not have as much time to spend on looking attractive as before. Empathy and patient understanding are virtues that no marriage can flourish without.

This business of patience really leads us on to the next important quality in a marriage - *trust*. If you do not fully trust your partner, then your marriage is already failing. Worse, if you happen to know for certain that they *will* let you down, or do something you will not like, then they are deliberately attacking the foundations of your relationship.

Life-partners should have a *faithfulness* towards each other that no-one can challenge - whether another woman or man, or a member of the family, or a person at work, or at the mosque. In the world outside people will say and do all sorts of things for all sorts of motives; often they try to upset a happy marriage for no other reason than it is happy - this being a form of destructive jealousy. If you *know* your partner fully, and know their character, then you should be able to trust implicitly that they will not behave in a manner that would let you down, and that if they are accused of having done this, then the accusation is false.

Even, if the worst came to the worst, and the accusation was *not* false, and on this occasion your spouse had let you down, if you trust your partner you will know that he or she will be bitterly regretting it, and wishing things could have turned out differently. The kindest thing in this situation in Islam is to 'cover the fault' of your loved one, and set it aside, giving them a chance to repent and not repeat the misdemeanour. 'Whoever conceals [the misdeed of] a Muslim, Allah shall conceal his misdeeds on the Day of Arising.' (Hadith narrated by Bukhari)

It is in keeping with the mercy of Allah that you should deal gently with them. If you were severe with them, or harsh of heart, they would have dispersed from round about you. So pass over their faults, and ask forgiveness for them. (Holy Quran, 3:159)

None of us is perfect. None of us can claim never to have done or said something that we did not later regret. The most beautiful thing about Islam in everyday life is its mercy and compassion - and the knowledge that when we are sorry for the things we have done wrong, or the things we have not done that we ought to have done, that our Lord forgives us.

O My servants, who have transgressed against their own souls! Do not despair of the mercy of Allah! Truly, Allah forgives all sins; He is Oft-Forgiving, Most Merciful! (Holy Quran, 39:53)

In Islamic marriage, we should try to act by these same principles, and always give our partners the fullest opportunity to make amends for their mistakes, trusting that their Islam is strong enough for them to live according to this principle.

The Blessed Prophet (ﷺ) explained:

Believers are like one body; if one member aches, the other members ache for it with fever and sleeplessness. (Bukhari and Muslim)

'The Muslims are to each other like the structure of a building. Each part of it gives support to the others.' Then the Blessed Prophet intertwined the fingers of one hand together with the fingers of the other. (Bukhari)

All of this is not just a generalised teaching to all the Muslims; it is especially important to Muslims who happen to be married to each other.

4 *A Sign and Foretaste of Paradise*

'*Nikah* (marriage) is my *Sunna*. He who shuns my *Sunna* is not of me.'

(Hadith from Muslim)

With these famous words, the Blessed Prophet left his followers in no doubt of his own personal approval of marriage, and, since his way of life was to be 'the Quran walking', we know that the sexual relationship really is the will of Allah for His subjects. It is worth stressing this point, for some people have a tendency to turn away from the 'things of the flesh', and regard the pleasures of marriage and sexual fulfilment as if they were self-indulgent evils!

As is well known, the Christian Church has had a tradition of asceticism which encouraged men and women to give up their sex lives in order to concentrate on their prayers and piety.

As is also very well known to older people, many ordinary men and women who fall a long way short of sainthood would also like to be able to give up their sex lives too, not for religious reasons but because they have proved so traumatic and disappointing and humiliating. Many people find the whole subject of sex dirty and degrading, and their unfortunate experience so unpleasant and unfulfilling as to reinforce these notions.

This is not the attitude to sex revealed to Muslims through the Blessed Prophet (ﷺ). There is nothing in Islam which encourages

31

shame of the sexual urge. As Allah Himself has made clear, He has created life-forms in pairs, including the human couple. When something is created as one of a pair, it is clearly incomplete without the other. It takes only the most rudimentary knowledge of biology to notice that male and female forms were created to 'fit together', like a jigsaw puzzle, and when things are as they should be, the moments when they do so 'fit together' are moments of great love, joy and fulfilment. As one of the ulema has affirmed:

> 'Sexual intercourse provides pleasure and energy, it refreshes the soul, banishes sorrow, anger and dark thoughts, and is a prevention of many diseases.'
> (Zabidi, *Ithaf al-Sada al-Muttaqin*, V, 371)

More than that, Islam teaches that in the act of sexual union and fulfilment there is a sign of Allah's greatness and compassion, and of His relationship with all humanity that turns to Him.

> 'A Muslim man can acquire no benefit after Islam greater than a Muslim wife who makes him happy when he looks at her, obeys him when he commands her, and protects him when he is away from her in herself and in his property.' (Nasa'i)

> 'The most perfect believer in faith is the one whose character is finest and who is kindest to his wife.' (Tirmidhi and Nasa'i)

In all these statements the Prophet (ﷺ) is addressing men; just as the Quran usually uses grammatically masculine expressions. However, the ulema say that this does not mean that the comments are exclusively meant for the male sex: by extension the same ethos is encouraged in women. Allah has made it quite clear in verse 33:35, for example, that the basic moral instructions of Islam are given to both men *and* women.

The Prophet (ﷺ) set a wonderful example of a husband devoted to his womenfolk, and in his case he had more than one wife to consider. He did not marry until the age of 25, and then remained content with the one wife until she died 25 years later. When he was over 50 he married other women, and when he died at the age of 64 his household included many women, who all loved him very much.

A Sign of Paradise

It is amusing to read the words of eccentric writers who are embarrassed by the thought that the Blessed Prophet could have been a fulfilled and happily married man, insisting that these wives of his middle age were all taken on out of pity and charity, most of them past the age of any interest in a sexual relationship. As it happens, the only wife the Prophet (ﷺ) married who we are certain was older than himself was his first wife, Khadija, who gave birth to six of his children when she was already over the age of forty, and who shared his bed and enjoyed the comfort of his arms to the exclusion of all others until she was 65! All the other wives, except possibly Sawda, were younger, and their stories will be considered in the next chapter.

Sa'id ibn al-Musayyib recorded the Blessed Prophet's opinion of a loving sexual relationship as follows:

'When a Muslim man intends to come to his wife, God writes for him 20 good deeds and erases from him 20 evil deeds. When he takes her by the hand, God writes for him 40 good deeds and erases from him 40 evil deeds. When he kisses her, God writes for him 60 good deeds and erases from him 60 evil deeds. When he comes into her, God writes for him 120 good deeds. When he stands up to make the ablution, God boasts of him to the angels and says: "Look at My servant! He stands up on a cold night to wash himself of impurity (janaba) seeking the good pleasure of his Lord. I bear witness to you that I have forgiven him his sins".'
(Maybudi, Tafsir, 1, 610)

The scholar Maybudi goes on to point out the importance of human beings granting their rights to each other. God, as Creator and Sustainer, has rights over all of us, but He so often tempers His divine Justice with His divine Compassion, and so forgives and forgoes His rights. Human beings, on the other hand, are required to be just towards one another, and if they have transgressed against any other person, to realise that Paradise is withheld from them until the claimant against them is satisfied.

The Messenger of God (ﷺ) once said: "Do you know who is the bankrupt?" and we replied: "The bankrupt among us, O Messenger of God, is he that has neither dirham nor dinar to his name, nor any property." But he said: "The bankrupt of my Umma is he

33

that shall come forward on the Day of Arising with the Prayer, the Fast and the Zakat, but having insulted this person, and abused that person, and having consumed another's wealth, and shed another's blood, and struck yet another. Each one of these shall be given a portion of his good works, and should these be exhausted before his obligation is discharged, then he shall be assigned some of their sins, which will be heaped upon him. Then he shall be cast into Hell."' (Muslim)

The Blessed Prophet stressed so often that men must be careful to consider the rights of all Muslims, which includes their women, and not just their male brethren and friends. It is so easy for some husbands to forget that their wives are the people they are perhaps *most* likely to insult, abuse, consume the wealth of, or strike. Muslim men must not overlook the rights of their wives, or forget that their lapses will be recorded against them in their 'Record'. The Prophet (ﷺ) taught:

'I counsel you to be kind to your wives, for they are your helpers. You have taken them only as a trust from God, making their private parts lawful through a word.' One day Umar ibn al-Khattab said: 'O Messenger of God, what should I take from this world?' And he replied, 'Let each of you take a tongue that remembers God, a heart that thanks Him, and a wife who has faith.' (Maybudi, I, 613)

The Prophet (ﷺ) placed a pious and worthy wife next to remembrance and gratitude to God. Imam Maybudi comments that one of the blessings of having a beloved and worthy spouse is that it allows a man more time to be free to engage in the work of the next world.

'When you keep to your worship,' he observed, 'if a boredom should appear such that the heart is wearied and you should fall behind in worship, looking at her and witnessing her gives intimacy and ease to the heart. That power of worship will then return, and your desire to obey God will be renewed.'

The author can bear witness that, as usual, the same applies when a wife can look with love upon a pious husband!

A Sign of Paradise

For Muslims, the Blessed Prophet is by definition the most perfect human being and the most perfect male. His love for women shows that the perfection of the human state is connected with love for the opposite sex, and this is part of love for God. If we cannot love the beings that we have seen and amongst whom we live, how can we claim to love Him Whom we have not seen, and Who lies beyond our powers of understanding?

> 'Three things of this world of yours have been made beloved to me: Women, and perfume, and the delight of my eye has been placed in the *Salat*.' (Nasa'i and Ibn Hanbal)

Some pious folk try to insist that the sexual act should only be indulged in for the procreation of children, and not simply because it gives pleasure. This is not what is taught in Islam. In fact, Islam teaches that the joy given in the marital act is a sign of what is to come, a foretaste of the joy of Paradise. This is proved by the fact that the inhabitants of Heaven have sexual relations simply for pleasure, and not for the procreation of children.

> 'They shall dwell forever with what their souls desired.' (Quran, 21:102)

> 'You will not have true faith till you love one another.' (Muslim.)

> 'My love is obligatory for those who love each other for My sake.' (*Hadith Qudsi* in Malik, *Muwatta'*)

> 'Love for women is one of the things through which God favoured His Messenger (ﷺ); for He made him love them in spite of the fact that he had few children. Hence the desired goal was nothing but the marriage act itself, like the marriage act of the people of the Garden, which is strictly for pleasure and not for producing offspring.' (Ibn Arabi, *Futuhat*, II, 193)

Occasionally, men argue that love of women is sinful because it distracts them from God. But would that which drew him away from God have been made lovable to the Blessed Prophet? Of course not. He loved only that which drew him closer to his Lord! In fact, a good woman is a source of *iḥsān*; she is a fortress against

Satan, and helps a man to keep to the Straight Path. The caliph Umar said: 'After belief in God, a man can have no better gift than a virtuous wife.' And Ibn Mas'ud used to say: 'If I had but ten days left to live, I would like to marry, so as not to meet God as a celibate.' This love that the Prophet (ﷺ) bore for women is *obligatory* for all men, since he is the model of perfection whose *sunna* it is the duty of Muslims to try to copy in their own lives.

5 *The Blessed Prophet and his Wives*

'And We sent messengers before you, and We assigned to them wives and offspring.'

(Quran, 13:38)

It is well-known to all Muslims that the wives of the Blessed Prophet, the 'Mothers of the Believers', were saints. In fact, they might usefully be compared to the twelve Disciples of Jesus (ﷺ) because of their closeness to him and their role in spreading his teaching. But it is also true that they were conspicuously happy and fulfilled human beings. Some people misguidedly take the point of view that sex is basically worldly (and not a blessing of Allah), and that the Prophet (ﷺ) was not interested in it, and all his marriages were contracted for purely pious or political reasons, in order to look after unfortunate widows or war captives. But this is no more than a half-fact, applying to only a few of his wives. One can only seriously hold the mistaken view that it applies to all his later spouses if one has not read the hadiths! Anyone who *has* studied the authentic collections of hadiths can see straight away that these are the thoughts of the type of Muslim that the Blessed Prophet actually disapproved of - those who would really prefer to be celibate. 'The worst among you are your bachelors!' (Hadith from Abu Ya'la and Tabarani.)

Allah has taught that the foundation of society is marriage, and that marriage, along with physical intimacy, was the Prophet's way.

Others, equally misguided, read about the number of the Prophet's marriages and assume that he was some kind of sexual athlete, and wonder how a man with such an appetite can be seen as one of the great Prophets. This again betrays ignorance, for most of the Prophets that came before him of whom we know also had many wives: Abraham, for example, had three, Jacob had four, David had thirteen, and Solomon had three hundred, plus seven hundred concubines! None of this implied that they were not real Prophets, or were obsessed with sex at all; it was the normal practice of good men to take into their households more than one woman if they could afford this. It was regarded as a generous practice!

The Prophet (ﷺ), by contenting himself with the love of one wife for twenty-five years, was considered positively abstemious! After the death of Khadija he went on to marry many other women; but as we have seen, he did not take a second wife until he was over fifty, and the ladies who subsequently shared his life were not all tempting young beauties, but women with stories of their own.

We will note in passing here their names, and their ages and status when they married the Prophet (ﷺ): **Sawda** bint Zumu'a ibn Qays (widow of Sakran, aged 55); **A'isha** bint Abi Bakr (virgin bride aged about 6); **Hafsa** bint Umar (widow of Khunais ibn Hudhayfa, aged 19); **Zaynab bint Khuzayma** (divorced by Tufail ibn Harith, and widow of his brother Ubaida, aged about 30); Hind bint Abu Umayya (**Umm Salama**, the widow of Abdullah ibn Abu'l-Asad her cousin, the Prophet's foster-brother, aged either 25 or 29); **Zaynab bint Jahsh** (daughter of Amina, the sister of the Prophet's father Abdullah, divorced by Zaid the freeman, aged about 39); **Juwayriyya** bint Harith (real name Barra, widow of Musaffa ibn Safwan, aged about 14 or 17); Ramla bint Abi Sufyan (**Umm Habiba**, widow of Ubaydullah ibn Jahsh, aged 36-37); **Safiyya** bint Huyayy (real name Zaynab, a Jewess, divorced by Salm ibn Mish-kam al-Qurazi the poet, widow of Kinana ibn Abi'l-Huqayq, aged about 17); **Maymuna** bint al-Harith (real name Barra, divorced by Amr, the widow of Abd al-Rahim ibn Abd al-Uzza, aged 51; her father's wife Hind ibn Awf was the sister of the Prophet's uncle al-'Abbas's wife Umm Fadl); **Raihana** bint Shamum, a Jewess, the widow of al-Hakam al-Qurazi, age unknown but young). There is said to have been another wife, whom the Prophet divorced, either called Aliya bint Zabyan or Qayla bint al-Ash'ath.

Of these ladies, it is clear that even if their marriages were political or undertaken for social reasons, the Prophet (ﷺ) physically loved A'isha very much, and also enjoyed the embraces of the four 'beauties': the aristocratic Umm Salama, his cousin Zaynab, and two daughters of defeated enemies - Juwayriyya bint al-Harith, and the Jewish woman Safiyya. He must also have enjoyed intimacy with his Coptic Christian Marya (scholars are not united on whether she was wife or concubine), because she gave birth to his son Ibrahim shortly before he died.

Only young people can suppose, anyway, that it is impossible for women over forty to be interested in physical intimacy. Middle-aged women who have had a miserable and unfulfilled life with selfish husbands are probably quite glad to give it up, but those with thoughtful husbands would be very sad to set a 'sell-by date' on their intimate life. Incidentally, it is worth pointing out to those who think the Prophet (ﷺ) cannot have had a physical relationship with the older ladies that Khadija did not marry the Prophet (ﷺ) until she was over 40, and yet kept him satisfied until she was 65, and gave birth to most of his children.

The Blessed Prophet was not a wealthy man and did not marry young. His first wife, **Khadija bint Khuwaylid,** was in fact his employer - a wealthy and intelligent widow who ran her own business, and herself proposed matrimony to the devout and highly thought-of young merchant, seeing in him the sort of man that she admired. She had been married twice before, with children from both marriages.

It is evident that they were both exceedingly pious people, even before the Prophet's call to Apostleship, and that they had the admiration for each other that could easily become love. The Prophet had worked as the overseer of her caravans for quite some time, and they knew each other well. The age factor appears not to have come into it. (The present author has seen fifty summers go by, and is at present blessed by the love of a pious man twenty years her junior, has faced exactly the same criticisms, and can so speak with gratitude for the gracious, brave and open-minded example of our dear Prophet!)

Later, the Prophet (ﷺ) made it quite clear that when people were considering matrimony, they should not marry for looks, or wealth, or rank, but for compatibility and piety. That was what counted; it was the force that would overcome the obstacles, and would make or break the marriage.

> Abdullah ibn Umar reported that God's Messenger (ﷺ) said: 'Do not marry only for a person's looks, for their beauty might become a cause of moral decline. Do not marry for the sake of wealth, as this may become a source of sin. Marry rather on the grounds of religious devotion.' (Tirmidhi)
>
> A man said to al-Hasan al-Basri: 'Several suitors have asked for my daughter. To whom should I give her in marriage?' He replied: 'To him who fears God the most. For if he loves her he will respect her, and even if he comes to dislike her he will not be cruel to her.' (Al-Ghazali)

To fall in love with someone simply because of their looks is dangerous and misguided for many reasons. Firstly, those good looks might conceal less pleasant sides to their character to which 'love is blind'. Later, because of the obsession with the partner's looks, the enamoured partner might be influenced into doing or accepting all sorts of wrong conduct in their desperation to keep their love of their 'idol'. Thus, those good looks might even cause a form of *shirk* in the heart of the one desperately in love with them!

Secondly, the good-looking person might be perfectly decent and good, but unfortunately the good looks begin to deteriorate with age, or increasing fatness, or damage through accident or illness. What then? If the lover only wanted them because of their looks, the relationship is now on tricky ground. The wise Prophet advised having more secure foundations for marriage than being carried away by a person's face or figure.

In fact, Khadija was a remarkable woman. She loved the Blessed Prophet until she died, was his first convert, and became his comforter through many crises.

'Whom shall I appeal to?' he asked her one day, during one of the long conversations that they had each time the angel Gabriel appeared to him. 'Who will believe in me?' Happy to see that he no longer doubted his new mission, Khadija exclaimed, 'At least you can call on me before all others. For I believe in you!' The Prophet

(ﷺ) was very joyful, and recited the *shahada* to Khadija, and Khadija believed. (Tabari, *Annals*, II, 209.)

He never took another wife while she lived, and even after her death he never forgot her or ceased to love her. Their marriage had lasted twenty-five years.

There are several touching traditions which show the Prophet (ﷺ) being deeply affected and moved to tears when he heard her sister Hala's voice, which sounded so much like hers, or saw something which had once belonged to her.

The Prophet's next beloved, A'isha, recorded:

> 'Although I had never met Khadija, I was never more jealous of anyone than her.' Once, when Khadija's sister Hala came to visit the Prophet (ﷺ), and called from outside for permission to enter, he trembled, being reminded of Khadija, for the two sisters had very similar voices. 'It must be Hala,' he said. A'isha said, 'Why do you keep thinking of that elderly woman who has been dead for so long, when Allah has given you such good wives?' 'No, no, no,' the Prophet (ﷺ) answered, 'I was given no finer wife than her. She believed in me when everyone else belied me; when they denied me she became a Muslim; when no-one would help me, she was my help. I had my children from her.' And he asserted, 'Allah gave me my love for her.'

After that, A'isha resolved never to take hurt from Khadija's memory.

He grieved for her for a long time, and was eventually persuaded to take other wives by his friends, and especially by his aunt Khawla, who was distressed to see him so sad and lonely. Khawla visited him one day and found him getting on with the domestic chores, washing the dishes with his four young daughters. Moved to pity, she urged him to take a companion to look after his household affairs.

When he did finally remarry, at first love did not enter into it. Like most leaders in Arabia in his day, he chose his next two wives for practical and political reasons rather than for their sexual charms. **Sawda** was an old friend, one of the first Muslims, and the widow of his friend Sakran, the brother of Suhayl. She was a homely, chubby, tall woman slightly older than himself - he was fifty-two, she fifty-five - the ideal person to look after his domestic arrangements and bring up his four motherless daughters. **A'isha**, his third wife, was only a little child, the daughter of his best friend. By marrying them the Blessed Prophet forged important links of kinship with the tribes of Suhayl and Abu Bakr.

Later, of course, we know that he came to love A'isha very much indeed, and when she became old enough the relationship became physical. He was never particularly attracted to Sawda, on the other hand, although they were good friends; later, she was quite content to let A'isha have 'her' night with him.

Those who are surprised that the Prophet (☙) could marry a six year old child forget that it was quite normal in both Arab and Jewish society for betrothals to be made for tiny children, even at birth, and for the little girls to enter their future husbands' households long before their marriages were consummated. One presumes that it was precisely this arrangement that Joseph the Carpenter of Nazareth undertook when he lived with the Virgin Mary, mother of Jesus (☙). Physical intimacy would not begin until the girl was old enough, usually at around the age of thirteen to fourteen, as in A'isha's case.

Once, the Blessed Prophet's companion Amr ibn al-As asked him which person he loved most in the world, expecting him to name one of the heroic young warriors. To his surprise, the Prophet replied straight away: 'A'isha'. (Zarkashi, *al-Ijaba*, 52.)

A'isha herself recorded a touching detail that indicated his love: 'After I ate one part of the meat on a bone, I used to hand it to the Prophet (☙), who would bite the morsel from the place where I had bitten. Similarly, when I used to offer him something to drink after drinking a part, he would drink from the place I had put my lips.' (Muslim.)

Like Khadija, A'isha gave the Blessed Prophet full support in his life of prayer and submission to God, frequently standing behind him through his long nightly hours of meditation, praying with him, and ready to give him whatever aid he needed when he had finished. His daily needs were very little - he lived so simply and ate so sparingly. The burden of this ascetic life fell on his womenfolk, who all shared his regimes. This would certainly not have suited every woman; the wives who married the Blessed Prophet were expected to be of like mind to himself, devout and self-sacrificing, living the life of the poorest folk of Medina.

It is therefore to her immense credit that A'isha had the full confidence of the Prophet (ﷺ) during his lifetime. This has allowed us to receive a wealth of information on private and intimate aspects of his *Sunna*, as we will see later. No-one apart from Khadija knew him as she did, she who shared his most intimate moments and private devotions; but, unlike Khadija, A'isha left a treasure of thousands of hadiths!

The Blessed Prophet appreciated her high intelligence and deep understanding, and he found her a worthy co-worker for Allah. He used to tell the Muslims that if they had any religious problems while he was absent from Medina, or needed any information, they could go for advice to A'isha.

After his death, the Muslims used to go to her for verification of what they had heard, confident of her judgement, not only because of her closeness to the Blessed Prophet, but also because of her own recognised abilities.

> Ibn Ata said: 'A'isha was, among all the people, the one who had the most knowledge of *fiqh*, the one who was the most educated, and compared to those who surrounded her, the one whose judgement was the best.' (Ibn Hajar, *al-Isaba*)

It is interesting to record that on one occasion she heard Abu Hurayra repeating a hadith concerning what the Blessed Prophet used to do after he made love. She disputed the details, crying: 'But who has heard that from Abu'l-Qasim'? (a name of the Prophet). The point was that Abu Hurayra was relying on hearsay, whereas she had had the experience of sharing the Blessed Prophet's most intimate times.

She had a keen mind and memory, and no fewer than 2,210 hadiths are narrated on her authority. In an age when the tribal elite found it difficult to accept the full significance of the Islamic teaching on female dignity, her reliability and the respect in which she was held formed a much-needed precedent for later generations of Muslim scholars.

For example, when according to Ibn Marzuq someone invoked in front of her a hadith stating that the three causes of the interruption of prayer were dogs, asses and women, she rounded on him smartly with the words: 'Now you compare us to asses and dogs! In the name of Allah, I saw the Prophet (ﷺ) saying his prayers while I was there, lying on the bed between him and the *qibla*, and in order not to disturb him, I did not move!' (Bukhari.)

She never accepted a hadith that was at variance with the Holy Quran, even if it came from so reliable a source as the son of the Caliph Umar. Human beings, no matter how high their rank, were all capable of making mistakes. Once Umar's son related a hadith about dead persons suffering punishment on account of the wailings of the mourners. She explained that he had misunderstood or misheard; no person in the Hereafter suffers for the misdeeds of the living. The Blessed Prophet had been commenting on the burial of a Jewess, and pointed out that her relatives were wailing while she was being punished. Ibn Umar conceded the point.

The Prophet's next wife was **Hafsa**, the daughter of Umar, whose husband Khunays had died from wounds suffered at the Battle of Badr when she was nineteen years old. Umar instantly approached their friend Uthman, who had just lost his own wife, the Prophet's daughter Ruqayya. However, Uthman did not rush to marry her, and neither did Abu Bakr, to whom she was also mentioned. It is possible that their reluctance might have been because the lady, like her father, had a fiery temperament.

The Prophet (ﷺ), realising Umar was hurt, offered to marry her himself. Hafsa was highly educated and very intelligent, and spent much of her time reading and writing. She also frequently argued points with the Blessed Prophet, a habit for which her father rebuked her, but which the Prophet responded to with gentleness. A'isha said of her: 'Hafsa is the daughter of her father. She is strong-willed like him.'

Perhaps in recognition of her strength of character, it was to Hafsa that the written text of the Holy Quran was given for safekeeping, and this was later recognised as the standard and authentic version against which all others were checked.

The Blessed Prophet did not turn away from women who were strong or argumentative or full of character - women like Khadija, A'isha, Hafsa or Umm Salama. In fact, he admired and loved them. The hadiths show that his wives were not disappointed, meek, downtrodden, shadowy, boring figures, there simply to do his bidding; on the contrary, his household was full of laughter, his

44

women spoke up whenever they were upset about something (on their own behalf or on behalf of others), and their quarters sometimes rang with female outrage and arguments. The Blessed Prophet's friends were sometimes frankly amazed that he did not discipline his wives as they expected!

Many new Muslims found this very perplexing, especially Hafsa's father Umar, who on occasion found the relaxed freedom granted to Muslim women difficult to accept.

> Umar said: 'By Allah, in the *Jahiliyya* (pre-Islamic age of ignorance) we did not pay attention to women until Allah revealed concerning them that which He revealed, and assigned for them that which He has assigned!' (Bukhari)

> 'Once, when I was pondering a certain matter, my wife told me she wanted me to do such-and-such a thing. I asked her what it had to do with her. Whereupon she said: "How strange you are, son of al-Khattab! You don't want to be argued with, whereas your daughter Hafsa argues even with Allah's Messenger (ﷺ), so much that he remains angry for a full day!"'

Umar went round to check the unpalatable facts with his daughter. To his chagrin, he found that his wife had spoken the truth. Furious with Hafsa, he warned her never to do it again. Then he went to the house of another of the Blessed Prophet's wives Umm Salama, who was also his relation, and spoke of it again. She, however, rounded on him and rebuked him:

> 'O son of al-Khattab! It is astonishing that you interfere in everything! Now you even want to interfere between Allah's Messenger (ﷺ) and his wives!' (Bukhari)

The Blessed Prophet's fifth female 'apostle' was **Zaynab bint Khuzayma**, a lady of outstanding piety and self-sacrifice, whose husband was martyred at Uhud, leaving her poverty-stricken and alone. After her marriage she was called 'Umm al-Masakin', the Mother of the Poor, for her generosity to the destitute. Once, when a poor man came to her house to ask for food, she had only flour enough for one meal, but gave it to him and went without herself. The Blessed Prophet deeply admired her, but tragically she died only a few months after their marriage.

45

Umm Salama (Hind bint al-Mughira) was the widow of his cousin Abu Salama. She was the mother of four children, who was twenty-nine years old when he married her. At first she was reluctant to marry him, not because she did not like him, but because she had been deeply in love with her husband, was pregnant with his last child, and did not know how she would adjust to being a co-wife. She had already turned down both Abu Bakr and Umar, who had offered to take her in.

The hadiths reveal her shyness; when the Blessed Prophet first used to visit her after their marriage, she used to pick up her baby daughter, and the Prophet (ﷺ) would leave her so that she could feed her. It took the persuasion of her foster-brother, who found out about this, to persuade her to be at ease with the Prophet.

She was an intelligent woman and a good companion to the Prophet (ﷺ), and came to love him intensely. When he was dying, she prayed that God would take her or her whole family, if only He would spare him.

He often took her along with him on major campaigns, and she offered him valuable advice on several occasions (for example, it was she who suggested he make the sacrifice at Hudaybiyya when the Muslims were refused access to Makka). The famous ayats that mention the equality of male and female believers were revealed following her inquiry as to why it was the Quran rarely specified women believers. (See Sura 33:35.)

The Prophet's only 'cousin-marriage' was to the strong-willed **Zaynab bint Jahsh**, who despite her age of 39 is said by the historians to have been very beautiful. She had previously been brought up under the Prophet's supervision, and had eventually married his freed slave and adopted son Zayd. Although the marriage did not finally succeed, this was an example of people from very different social backgrounds becoming equal in Islam. (It is important to notice how the Prophet (ﷺ) had quite deliberately not recommended cousin-marriage as his Sunna. Although he did eventually marry this cousin, Zaynab was his seventh wife - a long way from being first choice.)

We do not know how old Zaynab was when she married Zayd, but the Prophet may have arranged this marriage because he feared

46

that she would never marry. It is possible that she had resisted marriage for so long because she had hoped to be married to her cousin, the Prophet (ﷺ), and may have been disappointed when she only married Zayd instead.

Following her divorce, the Prophet (ﷺ) was pressed to marry her himself, to resolve the situation. At this stage, he did not see how he could marry her, for he had regarded Zayd as his own son; but then Allah revealed a verse to confirm that an adopted son could never be considered in the same category as a blood relation, and the Prophet (ﷺ) was able to take Zaynab into his household.

It was on this particular wedding night that he became distressed when inconsiderate guests tactlessly stayed too long; the 'verse of the Hijab' was revealed that enabled him to separate his private quarters from public life, and gain a little privacy.

Juwayriyya was the daughter of al-Harith, the chief of the Mustaliq tribe. The tribe attacked the Muslims, but were defeated, and Juwayriyya was among the booty. She was allocated initially to al-Thabit ibn Qays. As the daughter of a chief, she did not wish to be the property of an ordinary soldier, and requested release on payment of ransom.

When Juwayriyya was brought to A'isha, A'isha said that her heart sank when she saw her, because she was so pretty. 'By Allah, I had scarcely seen her in the doorway of my room before I disliked her!' She recalled later: 'I knew he would see her as I did.'

Sure enough, the Prophet (ﷺ) asked to marry her, and Juwayriyya accepted Islam; thus the enemy tribe became an ally. But A'isha is said to have always nurtured a certain jealousy towards her.

The Prophet's marriage to **Umm Habiba** was very different. She was the daughter of Abu Sufyan, and hence the sister of the future caliph Mu'awiya, and the widow of the Prophet's cousin Ubaydullah ibn Jahsh, Zaynab's brother. Her mother Safiyya bint Abu'l-As was the sister of the father of the Blessed Prophet's dear friend and son-in-law Uthman. Ubaydullah had migrated to Abyssinia with her, but there had apostasized and became a drunkard. When he died, the Negus of Abyssinia was distressed for her, and contacted the Prophet, who agreed to marry her himself. The wedding was performed by proxy. There was also a tradition that the people of Medina requested the Prophet (ﷺ) to marry her for she was a staunch Muslim, one of the earliest converts. They wished to spare her returning to the care of her then unbelieving father Abu Sufyan.

Little is known about **Raihana** of the Jewish tribe of Banu Nadir. She was a prisoner-of-war seen by the Prophet, who offered to marry her if she accepted Islam. Some traditions claim that she never gave up her Jewish faith, and the Prophet (ﷺ) kept her as a maidservant. One day she did accept Islam, but by that time the verse limiting the number of wives had been revealed, and so he did not marry her. On the other hand, the historian Ibn Sa'd claims that he did marry her after liberating her. Ibn Ishaq states that she died ten years before the Prophet (ﷺ), so one can only say about her life story that Allah knows best.

Zaynab bint Huyayy, to whom the Prophet (ﷺ) gave the name **Safiyya**, was another Jewess, the seventeen-year old daughter of an enemy of the Muslims. Huyayy, the chief of the Banu Nadir tribe traced his ancestry from the prophet Harun (Aaron). Her husband Kinana had earned notoriety for burying alive the brother of Muhammad ibn Maslama, who subsequently killed him in reprisal. She was chosen as a maid from the war-booty by Dihya al-Kalbi, but as a chief's daughter she also requested a more honourable fate. The Blessed Prophet released her, and married her himself.

She is said to have been beautiful, and A'isha was again beset by a degree of jealousy. At first A'isha and the other wives made life difficult for her, agitating her with jibes. But the Blessed Prophet always took her side. When A'isha once said that she did not know what all the fuss was about since 'one Jewess is much like another', the Prophet rebuked her by saying: 'Do not speak thus, for she has entered Islam and made good her Islam.' When they taunted her about her father, the Prophet (ﷺ) taught her to reply: 'My father is Harun and my uncle is Musa.' Once, Zaynab refused to lend 'that Jewess' a camel, and the Prophet (ﷺ) defended the 'Jewess' by separating himself from Zaynab for several months. Safiyya became a close friend of the Prophet's daughter Fatima, and in due course she and A'isha did become friends. In fact, A'isha, Hafsa and Safiyya formed a kind of 'trio'. She never gave up all of her links with her Jewish relatives, however; and when she died she willed a third of her estate to her sister's son. Although this was criticised, A'isha insisted that the bequest be upheld.

The Prophet's final wife was the elderly widow Barra, the sister of the his uncle al-Abbas's wife, who wished to mitigate her sufferings, and see her well-placed. The Prophet changed her name to **Maymuna**. Her nephew was the famous warrior Khalid ibn al-Walid, who became a convert after the marriage.

When the Blessed Prophet was sixty years of age, Allah sent a revelation limiting the number of a man's wives to four (Quran 4:3); but as his existing wives had by now been declared Mothers of the Believers, he did not put them aside.

The Blessed Prophet was a human man, and his wives were human women. While their life together was focussed on prayer, fasting, and spiritual advancement, their house was not a silent monastery. They knew many of the hurts and griefs of married life as well as its joys. On two occasions there were major crises in his household: when A'isha was accused of adultery, and when he took Marya the Copt into his household.

The 'event of the necklace', which caused the Blessed Prophet so much grief, took place when A'isha, who had been accompanying the Prophet on a journey, got left behind by the caravan and was brought back by a young tribesman. This created consternation: those who disliked her influence with the Prophet (🕌) instantly accused her of adultery, and did not believe her when she explained thet she had been searching for her favourite necklace when the caravan moved on.

Outraged and heartbroken, A'isha left the Prophet's house and went to her parents, where she wept for two days. Her mother, Umm Ruman, tried to comfort her by pointing out that all beautiful women had to expect this kind of trouble. Her father, Abu Bakr, advised her to go back to the Prophet and be penitent. When the Prophet (🕌) saw her, he asked her to confess any sin, saying that even if she was guilty, God would forgive her.

With great dignity, she looked steadily at him and said she would never admit to something she had not done. Her duty was to show patience, and ask God for help. By the time she had finished speaking, the Revelation came and the Blessed Prophet was communing with God. Abu Bakr covered him with a mantle, while her mother waited fearfully for the result. When God confirmed her innocence, all three adults were overjoyed and relieved.

Although she was still only fourteen years old, she had become a proud and dignified Muslim woman, who represented the kind of wife who owed her allegiance to Allah alone. The Blessed Prophet did not resent this nor complain of it - for such was the teaching of Islam, and A'isha understood it well.

Any man who embarks on the adventure of polygamy knows that there will be tensions and stresses caused by the inescapable friction of more than one woman in the household. When the Muqawqis of Egypt sent the Prophet (ﷺ) two attractive Coptic Christian girls, the strain on the wives' selfless acceptance of their husband's wishes was considerable. Of course, taking a concubine was not regarded as in any way abnormal or wrong at the time; but any woman who loves her husband would feel disappointed if she felt that she had not been able to fill his loving thoughts entirely.

Tradition states that one of these girls, Shirin, was given to the Prophet's friend Hassan ibn Thabit, while the second, Marya, was taken by the Prophet (ﷺ) to Umm Sulaym. As with the case of Raihana, it is not certain whether or not the Prophet married her. Some argue that the Prophet (ﷺ) did not take concubines but only wives; but many books number the Prophet's wives as nine when he died, which would mean that Marya and Raihana were only concubines. Allah knows best. Ibn Abbas states that the Prophet (ﷺ) gave Marya a home with the Nafir tribe where he had some property, and she used to spend the summer there, where the Blessed Prophet would visit her.

Other traditions suggest that he visited Marya every day, and she soon became pregnant. None of the wives apart from Khadija had ever given the Blessed Prophet a child, although there is a tradition that A'isha once miscarried; and inevitably this caused stress. Tempers were strained, and about this time rows broke out

50

in the household concerning the sharing-out of the meagre items of war spoils that they were allowed to have. Umar heard the racket coming from the women's quarters, recognised the voices of A'isha and his daughter Hafsa, and was horrified. He was already worried that Hafsa was getting out of hand, and had told her to control her jealousy and accept the fact that she was not as beautiful as A'isha, and that if she provoked the Prophet (ﷺ) too much, he would cast her aside.

The women became so vociferous about Marya that the Prophet wearily promised not to go to her again. But things did not improve, and finally the atmosphere became so strained that the Prophet withdrew completely from all his wives, and went into seclusion.

The Muslim community was appalled, for this was no mere domestic crisis. Many political and tribal alliances would have been jeopardised if he divorced them.

At first the Prophet (ﷺ) refused to see even Umar, and when he finally admitted him to his room, Umar found him lying on a rush mat which had left marks imprinted on his cheek. In the end, the Prophet (ﷺ) received a revelation stating that he should give all his wives a free choice. The Verse of the Option (33:28-9) stipulated that they should either accept his terms and live the kind of Islamic life he required, giving him the time he needed for worship and the administration of the community, or, if they felt they could not do this, to take an amicable and blameless divorce.

The Blessed Prophet stayed away from his wives for a month. At the end of twenty-nine days, he ended his seclusion and went first to the house of A'isha, who greeted him with the words: 'O Allah's Messenger, you said you would not come back for a month, but there is still a day to go. Only twenty-nine days have passed. I have been counting them one by one.' The Prophet (ﷺ) pointed out that this month had only twenty-nine days. Then A'isha added: 'Then Allah revealed the Verse of the Option. And out of all his wives, he asked me first; and I chose him.'

He gave this option to all his wives. Part of the 'choice' involved abandoning sexual relations with several of the wives for whom there was no physical attraction. Although the Blessed Prophet was a vigorous man, he was over sixty; yet he also realised that he needed to be just to all his wives in his marital relationship. Far from accepting that this was perfectly all right, and that they should just put up with things and be grateful that he had at least given them a home, he took their physical needs into account and did something about it.

The wives for whom he had never felt any physical attraction were given the opportunity to be released from marriage with him if they wished. But so much did they respect and love him, that they all chose to re-establish their non-sexual marriages with him rather than leave him. Their words were given, and peace was restored.

The Verse of the Option did not mention Marya at all, but concentrated on the attitude of the wives to luxury and worldly goods. The 'apostle-women' agreed to sacrifice their material self-interest, and earned their titles of Mothers of the Believers.

Marya gave birth to a son, who was given the name of the great Ibrahim, perhaps in recollection of that Patriarch who had founded the Arab tribes through his son Ismail. The Prophet and all the Muslims rejoiced, for his only previous sons, who had been children of Khadija, had died in infancy. Tragically, the same fate was to befall little Ibrahim.

All this must have been particularly painful for A'isha, for of all the Prophet's wives, she seems to have been the only one who was childless. The others had all had children by their previous marriages. It seems that the Prophet (ﷺ) well understood her sense of 'emptiness', and the need to compensate, for he gave her the *kunya*-name Umm Abdallah, named after one of her sister's sons.

At the time of the Option the Prophet (ﷺ) asked her to reflect very carefully before she agreed to stay with him, and he advised her to consult her father for his opinion. She proudly refused to do so. She did not even have to think: she chose Allah and His Messenger.

There is no doubt but that A'isha was the Prophet's beloved, and that she genuinely loved him in the fullest sense. She used to stroke his hair with his favourite perfume, wash from the same bowl as him, drink from the same cup, and sleep wrapped in the same garment. His favourite position for relaxation was to lie with his head in her lap.

6 *The Good Husband*

'A believing man must never hate a believing woman; if he dislikes one trait in her, he will find another trait in her with which to be pleased.'

(Hadith in Muslim)

Respect can never be gained by simply telling someone to respect you. Respect has to be earned, by how you speak and how you act - in other words, through the total message of what you are.

It is absolutely vital in a good Islamic marriage that the wife respect her husband, otherwise the marriage is going to be a miserable business. Since one of the basic ground-rules of Islamic marriage is that the husband is the 'imam' and the head of the household, he has to *prove* himself worthy of that position.

It is not true that a Muslim wife is expected to obey her husband in every single thing he says - there is a very important proviso. If the husband attempts to order her to do anything that clashes with Islam, it is her duty NOT to obey him, but to point this out (tactfully and gently), and to change his orders!

Therefore, if the wife is to respect her man, he must do his utmost to be worthy of and to merit that respect.

Many women, particularly in these days of 'women's lib', wonder why it is that a man should even be considered as head of the household. Most women know that most men have very little to do with the housework and routine side of things; some of them leave all the financial control of day-to-day expenditure to their wives, and sometimes even more important financial planning. It is the

53

mother who usually has most to do with things as important and varied as training the children in good manners and sound belief and seeing that there is food to eat in the house, and things as trivial as seeing that there is a clean shirt, a pair of socks, that things are picked up and put away, that toilets get cleaned, and so forth.

Once women have learned how to cope with all this, many of them do not see why they should regard their husbands as the head of the household.

In Islam, this concession to the man is of vital importance. It is part of God's plan, part of His ordinance.

It was ordained long before the revelation to the Prophet Muhammad (ﷺ). It was stressed in Christianity as well: for instance in one Christian text we read: 'Let wives be in subjection to their husbands as if to the Lord, because a husband is head of his wife as Christ is head of the congregation.' (Ephesians, 5:22-24.)

In His final religion, Allah has requested that wives obey their husbands and pay them respect in every matter that does not conflict with His will. Indeed, the Holy Prophet once said that if it had been possible for him to order a human being to bow down to any other human being, he would have asked wives to bow down to their husbands! He could not ask this, of course, for only God has that privilege and right; but it pointed to his deep desire for a happy family relationship in which the husband was definitely the boss!

However, before wives close this book in irritation and accuse it of blindly supporting rampant male chauvinism (the view that men are always superior to women, because that is the way things are!), let us make it quite clear that chauvinism, and arrogance, and refusal to listen to the other's point of view, have nothing to do with Islam.

A good Muslim husband is not chauvinistic or arrogant, or puffed-up with his own opinion of himself. He is also under authority, don't forget - the highest Authority of all. That Authority has commanded him to be humble, modest, gentle, kind and compassionate. It has not required him to go bumbling around issuing orders right, left and centre, the whole object of which might seem to be to get out of doing work himself, or to see all the activities of the members of his household centred around his own comforts and pleasures.

The Good Husband

Muslim husbands have the Blessed Prophet himself as their example, and they are expected to try to be like him; and to the extent that they succeed in being like him, do we find the respect issuing naturally from their Muslim wives. The more civil and kind a Muslim is to his wife, the more perfect in faith he is, and the more worthy of being her leader.

Most men, when they first marry, have to learn how to take hold of that position of authority. They have usually not been in such a position before, but were merely young men in someone else's household. They may never have held the position of boss at work, or in the office, or in the factory. They may have little or no idea about 'public relations' exercises and tactics, and so may well go blundering into terrible staff revolts, strikes and other difficulties and dissatisfactions. The new husband has to realise that when he has just been promoted to a position of 'boss' of a household, he has to learn the skills, or he will encounter the same staff problems.

Let us consider a few of them. First and foremost, I suppose, the 'workers' like to see their boss being fair, honest and of sound judgement. These things are absolutely vital. The moment a boss is known to be unfair, incapable or dishonest he is in for big trouble. People will see nothing wrong in their own dishonesty, getting away with whatever they can. Honesty is the key. Without it, the rest of one's religion is worthless.

How can a wife truly respect her husband (or vice-versa), when she knows he lies, fakes illness, fiddles the tax returns, or even pinches things?

> 'People make long prayers to Allah although their food is *haram*, their drink is *haram*, and their clothes are *haram*. How can their prayers be accepted?' (Hadith in Muslim and Tirmidhi)

Imam al-Ghazali records:

> 'When a certain man went out of his house, his wife and his daughter would say to him: "Beware of illegal earning, for we can endure hunger and hardship, but we cannot endure the Fire."'

As for the incapable boss, once workers take the point of view that he is an idiot who is going to make a mess of things, they start looking out for themselves to make sure that they, at least, come out of it all right.

Next, the boss must never exploit his workforce, or expect unreasonable things of them. Loyal workers will labour way over and above the call of duty for a manager who is decent, just, and gives them fair reward. Once they begin to feel exploited, trouble starts. The first thought is usually to consider if it is worthwhile financially continuing in such a job, if one is slaving away all hours for a pittance, and others are getting preferential treatment over you, and so on. 'He who cheats us is not one of us.' (Muslim.)

There are so many forms of exploitation in the workplace. And there are so many in marriage. The husband who is 'out at work' from, say, nine to five, and then comes home and puts his feet up for the rest of the evening while his wife continues to work has forgotten something - she was also working nine to five, and very likely started long before that. This applies not only when the wife has a job outside the house, but also when she is working *in* the house.

Many men find this hard to grasp, for some reason. The simple way to prove it would be for the wife to leave him for a few weeks and let the household run down, as it would swiftly do; and then suggest that perhaps the husband should sort it out by hiring someone to come and take over the wife's jobs.

As we have seen (page 22 above), it was not the Prophet's *sunna* to sit back and watch his wives getting exhausted in his service.

The boss that really draws out loyalty from his staff is the one who shows his own self-sacrifice. He is prepared to get his hands dirty. He will not ask anyone to do what he would not be prepared to do himself.

> 'An employer should not ask a worker to do anything beyond his capacity. If that which the employer demands is necessary, then he himself should lend a helping hand to the worker.'
> (Bukhari)

He will not sit behind the closed door with his feet on the desk, but will be a worker alongside the other workers (bearing in mind his rank and job-differentials, of course). He will not exploit or abuse his staff, and - very important - he will pay them their due, justly and in good time.

The Good Husband

The Blessed Prophet was very clear on all this: 'Give the worker his wage before his sweat dries.' (Ibn Maja.)

Husbands usually understand all this as regards their place of employment, but many need to realise that the main worker within the family is the wife. She must *never* be taken for granted - for her payment is so often not money at all, but being noticed, appreciated, and loved.

Due to his imperfection and selfishness, there are many times when the husband, while wanting very much to be respected as the head of the family, fails to show the needed consideration and love to his wife, and thus 'shoots himself in the foot'.

No matter how much a man may actually love his wife, if he doesn't show it, she will not *feel* loved. No matter how much he does appreciate her, if he doesn't show it, she will not *feel* appreciated. She may deduce from his attitude that the only things that matter to him are his own pleasure and satisfaction.

> 'Among my followers the best of men are those who are best to their wives, and the best of women are those who are best to their husbands. To each of such women is set down a reward equivalent to the reward of a thousand martyrs. Among my followers, again, the best of women are those who assist their husbands in their work, and love them dearly for everything, save what is transgression of Allah's laws.'
> (Cited in Doi, *Women in Sharia*, 9)

What else makes bosses unpopular with the workers? When they are *domineering*. To gain respect, a man has to show himself steady and strong and able to take decisions, but that does not mean that no-one else is ever to be consulted, or that no-one else's opinion counts, or that the wife's opinion should never be seriously considered because it doesn't happen to agree with the husband's.

Of course, this does not mean that a husband has to put himself out all the time making himself a slave to his wife's wishes. A domineering wife is worse than a domineering husband! Moreover, wives do not usually appreciate a man who abuses his position of headship by leaving everything to her, and passing over to her all the decision-making. When that happens, the wife soon begins to wonder what use the husband is, and whether she might not actually manage better without him.

If the answer to the question, 'What is your husband for?' is along the lines of 'making a mess, creating chores and problems, filling up space, making you do things you don't want to do, and creating a lot of work you wouldn't have to do if he was not there', then sooner or later a woman is going to wonder why she is doing this - and the marriage is on the rocks.

> 'Men are the protectors and maintainers of women, because God has given the one more strength, and because they spend of their property. Therefore righteous women are the obedient, guarding in (the husband's) absence what God has guarded.' (Quran, 4:34)

The man has to show the protection, the maintenance, and the strength before he receives the obedience and the co-operation.

Just because a man is head of the household does not mean that he is issuing commands at every hour of the day. Usually it simply means that when the two of them at times disagree, and a row threatens, he has a casting vote. The husband does not always have to give in to his wife's wishes; but he is a fool if he does not listen to her reasons why she wants a certain thing doing, or wants it doing a certain way. Good Muslim husbands and wives both realise that everyone is capable of making mistakes, of not being perfect, and both should consider each other's rights and requests with an open mind and humility. The Prophet (ﷺ) emphasised this time and time again. A modern Nigerian scholar remarks:

> 'It is a fact, however, that sound administration within the domestic sphere is impossible without a unified policy. For this reason the Shariah requires a man, as head of the family, to consult with his family and then have the final say in decisions concerning it. In doing so, he must not abuse his prerogative to cause any injury to his wife. Any transgression of this principle involves for him the risk of losing the favour of Allah, because his wife is not his subordinate but she is, to use the words of the Prophet, the "queen of the house", and this is the position a true believer is expected to give his wife.' (Doi, *Women in Sharia*, 10)

Even if the man has more responsibility than the woman and therefore has a 'degree over her', this does not necessarily make him *better* than his wife.

How can you tell if you are being a good husband? What does a good husband have to do?

The Good Husband

Well, he has to be a good *provider*, to the best of his ability. Islam is very keen on men earning, striving and supporting, and not depending on others.

> 'What a man spends on his family is a *Sadaqa*, and a man will be rewarded even for the morsel that he raises to his wife's lips.' (Bukhari and Muslim)

> 'He is not one of us who possesses money but keeps his family away from his wealth.' (*Mustadrak*)

> A celibate man once told a scholar: 'God has given me a share in every good work', and he mentioned the Hajj, the Jihad, and so on. 'How far you still remain,' replied the scholar, 'from the work of the saints (*abdal*)'. 'And what is that?' 'Legitimate earning and supporting a family.' (Ghazali)

> 'Supporting a wife is not only a training and a discipline, but also a providing and a caring and a form of worship in its own right.' (Ghazali.)

A man's wife and family have material needs, and things cost money. It is a poor husband who keeps his pay packet to himself, if the wife has no independent financial means of support. It is very galling for most women to be forced to ask their husbands for a bottle of scent, or new underwear, or new clothes for the children, let alone adequate finances to buy the food and pay the bills.

Husbands should be alert to the cost of living, and make sure that the allowances they give their wives are reasonable. If the husband just hands over the barest minimum, and keeps everything else for his own pleasure, this is not fair. He can only do this by having a wife who is a slave-worker, and not a wife! Once again, it would be a good exercise for him to work out how much it would cost him to replace his wife with hired help.

Being a good provider also means that the husband should not waste his money, or fritter it away. Obviously a man cannot be blamed for being a poor man if it is not his fault; but he can be blamed for being idle, and greedy, and mean, and selfish. In the Western world, many wives are disappointed by husbands who waste their earnings on alcohol, gambling and 'nights out with the boys'. Muslim husbands should obviously not do this, but if the

59

husband innocently goes out three or four times a week to a hired sports centre, he should consider what he is allowing his wife for her relaxation, and whether his use of time and expenditure is fair. A wife who notices her husband spending all his time and money on things like indoor sports is not going to be very thrilled with him for long, as she sits at home alone darning the socks!

Muslims should learn to live within their means, and this is often difficult for a new husband and wife. It is so easy to get into debt, especially in modern societies that encourage you to 'live now, pay later'. Muslim couples should be awake to the fact that if they live foolishly and irresponsibly, they will indeed 'pay later', and not just in cash! The true believers are 'those who, when they spend, are neither prodigal nor miserly; and there is always a firm standing-place between the two.' (Quran, 25:67.)

At the same time, they must take care not to become materialistic. There are things which are more important than keeping up with the neighbours, and having all the latest expensive gadgetry and cars. Riches are a temptation and a snare. So many sayings of the Prophet (ﷺ) point this out:

> 'Riches are sweet, and a source of blessing to those who acquire them by the way; but those who seek them out of greed are like people who eat but are never full.' (Bukhari)

> 'It is not poverty which I fear for you; it is that you might begin to desire the world as others before you desired it, so that it destroys you as it destroyed them.' (Bukhari and Muslim)

> 'The love of money is the source of all wickedness.' (Bayhaqi)

> 'Richness does not consist in the abundance of worldly goods; richness is the richness of the soul.' (Muslim)

No matter what wonderful possessions a materialistic way of life may bring, they can never compensate for the pain of seeing family relationships weaken and break down. What is the point of spending so much time at work in order to gain the physical things of life that you have no time or energy left for the spiritual things? And no time or energy to build up love and compassion and friendship in your household?

The Good Husband

It is up to the husband, as head of the house, to be alert to this and make sure he is doing his spiritual and loving duty. Yes, he should work hard to provide the physical needs of his household; but he should put his ultimate effort not into riches and material things which will pass away, but into the service of God through loving his wife and family, teaching them, and building up their spiritual lives together.

> 'Nobody shall meet God with a sin greater than that of having left his family in ignorance.' (Imam Daylami)

It is vital to realise that this means praying together often, which is actually one of the things so appreciated by Muslim wives who, with the decline of the extended family, so frequently have to pray alone. It is such a lovely thing to kneel behind the head of your house, your husband-imam, and worship with him from time to time. However, your husband-imam must also bear in mind the principles taught by the Blessed Prophet himself, who made his prayers fit the needs and necessities and hardships of the congregation behind him.

> 'I stand up to pray and I intend to pray at length; but when I hear the cry of a child I shorten it for fear that the mother might be distressed.' (Bukhari and Muslim)

Prayer is not meant to be done out of duty or boredom, but out of love. The *fiqh* of Islam (carrying out the ritual details) is one aspect only; a no less important aspect is the inner dimension of faith, the *tasawwuf*, which brings spiritual insights and true devotion of the heart.

If a husband is obsessed only with the *fiqh* (outward) aspect, whereas his wife is drawn more towards the *tasawwuf* (inner) dimension, then here is an opportunity for the devil to creep in between them; for there is a natural tendency for each side to think that their own preoccupation is the best. The *tasawwuf* worshipper will have a loving awareness of God's presence throughout the day, and as well as performing the basic obligations will pray in short (or long) bursts of great personal devotion. The worshipper limited only to

61

the *fiqh* will regard it as beneficial to perform as correctly as possible, and earn merit, by increasing non-compulsory prayers and *rak'as*. But what Islam requires is that we combine the two. Both *fiqh* and *tasawwuf* are dangerous without each other: the inner form of the soul during the prayer and the outward arrangement of the body must be in harmony. The heart must prostrate as well as the body.

One fruit of this balanced spiritual activity will be that each spouse is able always to consider the hopes and faith of the other, and to be open-hearted.

One partner should not be so preoccupied with his or her own spiritual progress that they fail to show sincere concern for the other. If the husband does not give sufficient attention to his wife's spiritual needs, then in time she may no longer cherish the same goals that he does. If parents do not take enough personal interest in the spiritual growth of their children, they may find their hearts and minds being drawn away by the materialistic world which surrounds them. This will be almost inevitable unless they take the trouble to explain not only the 'whats' but also the 'whys' of Islam.

Finally, it is very important for a boss to show respect and honour to his workforce. They are not slaves - they are living beings with their own hopes and feelings, fears and frustrations.

This applies particularly to husbands honouring their wives in the sexual relationship, about which more will be said shortly. So much frigidity and lack of interest on the part of wives is caused by husbands who are ignorant of a woman's physical and emotional makeup. Some husbands are harsh and demanding, satisfy their own needs without considering those of their wives, demand sex when their wives are tired or feeling ill, or when they have earlier upset them and put them right out of the mood.

They have not grasped the words of the Blessed Prophet who counselled men not to leap upon their women like animals, but to 'send a messenger' first. He also used to say that a man who beat his wife like a slave during the day could hardly expect her to fall happily into his arms later that night. By a simple process of analogy, one must extend this hadith to those men who treat their women like slaves. The same applies: they will only gain disappointment and resentment, not love.

The Good Husband

Muslim men should obviously not look outside their own home for sexual enjoyment of any kind. If they did, that would certainly not be honouring their wives. The Prophet (ﷺ) wisely said on one occasion:

> 'Whenever any one of you comes across an attractive woman, and his heart is inclined towards her, he should go straight to his wife and have sexual intercourse with her, so that he might keep himself away from evil thoughts.' (Muslim)

The husband who honours his wife does not treat her as an inferior being. The Prophet (ﷺ) told men to feed their wives with the same sort of food as they received themselves (not obliging them to give them the best all the time, while the wife gets the left-overs!), and clothing them with the same sort of clothes - in other words, if the husband likes expensive and stylish things, he should not spend so much on himself that his wife is reduced to hunting around for cheap bargains and making do. The principle is fairness - yes, the husband may have earned the money, but the woman has made it possible for him, and she has rights over it.

> 'You shall give her to eat when you take your food, and you shall clothe her when you clothe yourself.' (Hadith from Abu Daud)

If the wife falls short of expectations, it is stupid to treat her harshly and make her life unpleasant. Try to improve matters by tact and gentleness and encouragement - as you would like others to do for you when *you* fall short. Don't start trying to run the kitchen or the household yourself, pushing her out of the way and making her feel embarrassed and small. Bosses who do that to their workers soon find their staff depressed and in revolt, and they usually walk out sooner or later. Far better to communicate, train gently, explain things, and make appreciative noises when things are going right.

> 'Whichever man is patient with the bad character of his wife shall be given a reward like unto that which Job shall receive; and whichever woman is patient with the bad character of her husband shall be given the same reward as Asiya, the (saintly) wife of Pharoah.' (al-Ghazali)

63

Love may be based on many things, but to be of true value it must go beyond mere human affection or mutual desire and be governed by what is for the highest good of the loved one. That kind of love can sometimes call for reproving or disciplining, just as a parent reproves or disciplines a much-loved child. But in Islam it is important to be long-suffering and kind. Even when a situation provokes you, and perhaps unfair accusations are being made, you must show restraint and generosity. Remember the saying: 'The true Muslim is like the earth: everything foul is thrown upon it, but only what is beautiful grows from it.'

True love is not impatient, or 'picky'. It is not jealous or suspicious or possessive. Those things are signs of insecurity, fed by the imagination, and should be watched out for. It is so easy to see other people's faults and failings, and so hard to acknowledge them in ourselves; but if we are good Muslims we must make the attempt. As a hadith says, 'Blessed is he who is so concerned by his own faults that he cannot see the faults of others.' (Daylami.)

True love does not behave indecently or with vulgarity. A good husband or wife does not discuss the shortcomings or intimate skills of their spouse with others, which would be so hurtful if found out. Nobody likes being laughed at, especially for things which are personal and private. The Blessed Prophet said:

> 'On the Day of Judgement, the lowest person in the sight of God will be the man who is intimate with his wife and then broadcasts her secrets.' (Hadith narrated by Muslim)

And Imam al-Nawawi says: 'Know that a husband should never discuss sexual matters with any of his wife's relatives.'

This principle applies even after a divorce. Imam al-Ghazali tells a story about a pious man who wanted to divorce his wife, and was asked: 'What have you against her?' He answered: 'A man of understanding does not reveal his wife's secret.' After the divorce, he was asked why he had divorced her, but he merely said: 'What business of mine is another man's wife?'

The good husband comes home from work tired, but he does not forget his duties and his love for his family. He may not be in the least eager to chatter, and needs to take rest - but his wife may have

64

been treasuring some detail to tell him all day; and whereas he may have been surrounded by adults to whom he could talk and enjoy conversation, she may have had no-one to talk to but the baby, the cat and the curtains! Honour the rights of your wife, and be kind.

And what about the children? If the father makes no time for them, and fails to teach them to respect their mother by his own attitude towards her and treatment of her, then sooner or later he will pay the price for it. Children need to *see* their parents' love and respect for each other, their united cooperation, and their willing-ness to help each other. Phrases like 'wait until your father gets home!' and 'Go ask your mother!' inevitably cast the person who has to do the disciplining, or has to say 'no', in the role of villain. If there is to be family happiness, each parent should receive the child's love and respect. On no account should mother and father allow a child to pit one against the other - a skill they pick up very easily, sad to say!

If children are expected to respect their parents, then the parents must live in such a way that they are deserving of respect, and provide a good example for the child to follow. Selfishness, bad temper, unreasonableness, laziness, dishonesty, abusiveness: these are all qualities swiftly picked up and copied by children. Earn respect by providing a peaceful and loving Muslim home, a good set of standards, a good and consistent example in your own conduct, sound training in manners and morals, and loving and gentle discipline when needed.

Children learn about love by seeing it, and they learn to give love by receiving it. Love cannot be bought. Neglectful parents may shower gifts upon their spouses and children, but to try to buy love only cheapens it. It is not gifts but your time, your energy and your love that are needed - giving, helping, serving, sharing.

Watch out for that big person-replacer, the TV screen. TV watch-ing and computer games can become an addiction which replaces doing and living with merely seeing - and most of that seeing is pretty rubbishy, especially mass-produced children's programmes! It also replaces talking together and playing together. In some cases, it even replaces communication while eating together! One day, you might switch the screen off, and find out that your whole family has changed, grown old, and maybe fallen apart.

65

Never underestimate the bonding value of the family meal. Sufyan al-Thawri said: 'I have heard that God and His angels bless a family that eats together.'

All human beings need some recognition, to be accepted and approved, to feel that they belong. To get those things, of course, the individual must bear in mind the whole group to which he or she belongs, and to feel valuable, they must contribute to it. Children must learn to take responsibility, to belong to and support the family, and eventually do things for themselves so that they will be able in due course to support their parents and set up families for themselves.

Finally, the little 'extra' touches can really lift up a humdrum relationship. The Blessed Prophet said: 'Even to put a morsel of food into your wife's mouth is a *sadaqa*' (Bukhari and Muslim). This indicates the kind of tenderness which should exist in a Muslim marriage. The squeeze, the arm around the shoulder, the touch of the hand, the pinch on the cheek, the little gifts that show you have thought about your wife during the day - these are the messengers that really get the message across.

> 'There is no woman who removes something to replace it in its proper place with a view to tidying her husband's house, but that Allah records it as a virtue for her. Nor is there a man who walks with his wife hand in hand, but that Allah sets it down as a virtue for him; and if he put his arm round her shoulder in love, his virtue is increased tenfold.' (Doi, *Women in Sharia*, 10)

No husband or wife is ever perfect; but when a husband shows love and thought for his wife, and acts in accordance with the principles of Islam, he will surely earn not only her love and respect, but that of Allah Himself.

7 *Celebrating the Difference*

'And the male is not like the female.'
(Quran, 3:36)

There is no doubt that when Allah created that 'single soul', and from it derived the first couple, Woman was not just a revised model of Man. And the differences, far from being the product of chance or random whim, were the wise and compassionate workings of our Creator, Who exquisitely designed each half of the pair to complement the other physically, emotionally, mentally and spiritually.

They had certain things in common - and an absolutely fundamental range of differences!

It is true that there are plenty of 'sensitive' men and 'coldly logical' women. Nevertheless, it does seem that when it comes down to working out the mechanics of helping men and women to live together smoothly as husband and wife, it is a good idea to remind the hopeful newlyweds that they are *not* the same at all - it is easier to solve a lot of the problems if one remembers the saying that 'women come from Venus, and men come from Mars'.

Just like visitors from two different planets, husbands and wives don't always 'speak the same language', or understand the same consequences from a course of action, or look at a problem through the eyes of someone from the same background.

Quite apart from the 'gender gap', which has been carved into the chromosomes of every single cell in the body, one obvious factor is that the two partners have come into their marriage from two different families, with entirely different past-tracks. Since experiences in childhood play so important a role in shaping our thinking and attitudes in adulthood, there will be unknown depths to deal with, and conflicting views will inevitably break surface from time to time. When both partners come from a very similar background, sharing the same religious beliefs and practices and aims, the problems are greatly reduced - but they are not done away with entirely. Much depends on what happened to them as individual boys and girls.

Men who get a frequent blasting of the repeat tunes: 'You don't love me!' 'You never listen to me!' 'You don't care how I feel!' need to ask themselves why it is that their wives are feeling so insecure. Are they really lacking in love, or not communicating that love? A wife who knows that she is very dear to her husband feels warm and safe inside. However, if a wife had a cold and inadequate father who did not give her adequate emotional support as a child, or one who despised his wife and treated her abusively as if she was a fool or a servant, then when she is 'off-guard', low and tired, she may have an overwhelming need for approval and reassurance that has nothing to do with her husband. The perplexed husband cries: 'But I could tell her I love her a hundred times, and it *still* wouldn't be enough!' This, unfortunately, is true - but understanding *why* might help alleviate his irritation and bafflement.

It is a good idea for husbands and wives to try to see each other from the perspective of *their* pasts, rather than their own. This is particularly important when the partner has been systematically humiliated and cruelly treated, or abused physically or sexually by a parent or guardian, or was unwanted.

You cannot undo the past, nor completely cure its effects; but you can do a very great deal to heal a distressed mate, or at least comfort them in love. Instead of downplaying the neglect or abuse, even though you may not have experienced it personally, you should not underrate their anguish, but acknowledge their past and give your support.

Therefore, it is only fair, of course, if the 'hurt' partner makes sure the other fully understands the problem, so far as he or she is able to communicate it. At a time when emotions are not heated, discuss your feelings, explain why you feel hurt and what you need in order to feel reassured.

Hurt people have such a natural tendency to summon up all the traumas from the past and use them as emotional weaponry when they get into arguments. Whenever you hear 'It's all your fault!', 'You should/shouldn't be able to do this!' or the deadly 'You *always/never* do/remember that!' you are probably dealing with a ghost from the past. Husbands or wives who use this kind of phraseology do not mean it really - the statements are provably not true - but there is an old accumulated 'hangup' of deep feeling here.

These husbands and wives should try to rephrase themselves assertively in terms of how *they* feel about whatever it is, rather than an accusation of what the other is or is not doing.

'When you do that, I feel unloved/misunderstood', is much more dealable-with than 'You don't love me' or 'You never understand me!' It is a very good idea to get out a book on basic assertiveness training, and have a look into its insights and skills. Most managers who work smoothly with their staff do this - they are sent on courses. It wouldn't hurt those trying to run a good, smooth marriage to know some of the same techniques.

For a wife to feel dearly loved, much more is required than just being pleased that she has been able to submit successfully to her husband's will. He could have a horse or a dog that is well-trained, submissive and never argues back. But people need *real* companionship and helpmates to work and live with. What a husband needs is a wife who not only loves and respects him but becomes also a real helper and genuinely supports him in the decisions he makes. This, of course, is not difficult when those decisions are arrived at following mutual agreement, and are on the right road of Islam.

Things are not quite so easy when you genuinely disagree. What then? Would your wife then do her best to make your decision work (provided it was not against the will of Allah), or would she hold back stubbornly, and hope to see you make a mess of it, and then enjoy the pleasures of 'I told you so'?

A good Muslim wife will not try to usurp her husband's headship of the family. Many women do, of course, and many of them succeed, wearing down their men through constant nagging or a constant display of their brilliant efficiency as opposed to the faults and inadequacies of their husbands.

It makes those women very difficult to live with, and it steadily erodes the woman's genuine respect for her man. Constant criticism generally produces an uncertain, indecisive husband. Don't you remember how those critical, humiliating teachers at school made their pupils feel? They didn't teach them much, but turned them into stupid kids who could never get anything right, who ended up either keeping their heads down or aggressively rebelling. Wives who can see nothing but their husbands' inadequacies need to remember how difficult it is for them to carry out their role as leader, and how easy it is to go wrong.

Providing the couple have arrived at their decisions with proper consultation and thoughtfulness, the wife should 'cover the faults' and weaknesses and mistakes of her husband and do her best to *boost* his confidence, not knock him down. Her loyalty and trust in him will all serve to strengthen him and ensure that he improves in skills and moves towards success. After all, a good Muslim man should be her best friend, not her enemy.

When friends disagree with one another, the decision-maker who proved to be wrong will soon dump any friend who crowed and laughed at him, or who continually tried to bring him down or belittle him.

This is another reason, of course, why a woman should be so careful when choosing a husband. She should take great care to marry the sort of man that she *is* going to respect and be able to obey without feeling dreadfully trapped or helpless or frustrated by *knowing* all the time that his leadership will not be up to scratch.

It can be dangerous when wives start to act like the husband's mother! 'Don't forget your briefcase!' 'You idiot - you didn't forget so-and-so, did you?' Once the husband starts to feel patronised and henpecked by this, he may revert to the little boy's longing to escape through the door and get out to play.

There is also the very real danger that he will really start to identify his wife with his mother, and since Mother probably spoilt him rotten, the wife may not come out of the comparison too well. Wives should remember the wise old saying - 'A man can love a hundred women, but he only has one mother'. Turn a wife into a substitute mother, and a husband might soon start wishing he had not swapped her for the 'real' one.

One regular flashpoint in marriage comes when the husband walks in to find a wife in tears, in a mood, angry, desperate with worry, or whatever, and he listens for a bit, decides it is trivial stuff, mutters something and then goes off to think about his own problems. Meanwhile, the wife explodes with the 'You don't love me!' and 'You don't listen to me!' What she has perhaps failed to realise is that his withdrawal has nothing to do with her, or anything she has said or done. He is still involved in his own fears, insecurities and pains, and perhaps even needs to 'lick his wounds'. He doesn't intend to worry her with *his* problems; so it seems doubly hard to be accused of not caring about *hers*.

It is usually a highly noticeable feature of a good marriage that when husband and wife meet each other again after a day apart, they greet each other properly, and pay attention to each other for a few moments. Husbands need to be aware that a perfunctory peck on the cheek does not count in the wife's eyes as 'paying attention', and may not satisfy a strong need she has for emotional reconnection.

Women are from Venus, the saying goes, and men are from Mars. When men listen, they usually do it swiftly, absorbing the information, working out what to do about it, assessing its importance. At work, many men prefer to work out solutions on their own, and discuss them only with those whose advice they really need. Some like to get away from the problem for a while, and return to it later. When they get home, they often appreciate solitude - and this is where many wives fail to show understanding and appreciation.

Some wives handle a man's need for peace and solitude badly. They intuitively sense the tension, and react by trying to get him to tell them what it is all about. The husband may find the thought of his wife knowing about it intrusive and humiliating, and may not wish to talk to her about it, but to keep her and his 'home haven' out of it. It would take far too long to explain all the ins and outs to her anyway, and he doesn't want to waste his evening. He doesn't want an hour of his wife mulling it over for him, he wants some peace. Yet, the more he backs off (either to get peace, or to think his problems through alone), there she is trotting behind him in hot pursuit, still pressing to know what's wrong and wanting him to talk about it.

When he manages to shut her up, or to escape, the wife feels hurt, unloved, and left out, partly because he has not paid any attention to *her* problems or appearance, or the food that she has got ready, and partly because he has not shared his worry with her. He has excluded her, as her friends would not have done. This must mean that he does not love her!

And the poor man, once he has had enough of chewing over the problem, turns back to the loving wife he had set on one side for the moment only to find her seething with resentment and full of hurt and anger. 'Men are from Mars; women are from Venus'.

Communication is vital. The man has to *tell* his wife that he needs some peace to think things through, and that of course he does love her, he just doesn't want to burden her with something from work. When she still cries words that mean 'But why? Aren't I your best friend?', then the best deflection of wrath is the kiss and the undivided attention he can give to *her feelings*. It doesn't have to be for long, just long enough for her to note it and acknowledge it.

A lot of husband-wife bickering happens not because they disagree, but simply because the man feels criticised and humiliated and that his wife disapproves of his point of view, while the wife disapproves of the way he is talking to her.

Let's just think about some good listening skills - another thing managers frequently learn on courses! Active listening is a way of making sure that both speaker and listener really understand each other. You have to pay careful attention, and pick out the important message (which may be underlying and not on the surface). Try to work out what *feelings* are involved, and acknowledge them. Try not to judge, criticise or dispute until you are sure of what the speaker really intended to put across. Let the speaker confirm that, and if you got it wrong, let them explain again. If what you are hearing is criticism, then don't boil over - there may be truth in that criticism, but it was simply unloaded on you in a way that was painful. Instead of just throwing the pain back on your critic, try to defuse the situation by acknowledging that you understand whatever upset feelings you may be held responsible for, and try to work out how you could improve the situation.

If you really feel that you are justified in a complaint, try to work out how you can best deal with it without starting a war. You may *feel* that your partner was being inconsiderate, thoughtless, unwise, arrogant, chauvinistic, etc., but probably he or she did not mean to be. State your feelings without making sweeping accusations, and try to phrase your comments as talk about yourself and not attacks on your spouse. Remember that 'the ego is always enjoining evil' (Quran, 12:53).

'When you did that, I felt ... ' This does not accuse your partner, but simply states how you felt. He or she cannot argue with that. They might be very surprised, since they probably never intended to upset you at all. If you simply charge in with 'You always' or 'You never', then the person being attacked will frequently just deny it or justify themselves, and the grievance for which you hoped to find a solution might be deflected into just another battle over an irrelevant detail of speech.

'Will you please stop harrassing me?' is an attack. 'When you did that, or said that, I felt very harrassed' is not. It is a statement that presents a problem to the other person, which he or she may be required to solve. When people *know* that particular actions or words have particular effects, then if they still persist in doing them, they will have to take responsibility for the result.

'When you always stay out with your friends, leaving me alone, or you don't come to bed until I'm asleep, it makes me feel very unloved. It shakes the love I feel for you, and I am beginning to feel resentment and dislike instead.'

Either the man will click into his work-mode of 'here is a problem to be solved, what must I do?' or he will not care less, in which case, why are you still married to him?

Sometimes the partner really needs to be told that if they keep on doing or saying something the spouse will not feel loved or wanted, and may indeed cease to love or want them. Take a personal and embarrassing example - suppose the husband regularly and thoughtlessly breaks wind in bed? She may be excruciatingly embarrassed, unable to speak to him about what she interprets as a fearful insult, and bitterly resent and hate it. If she does not tell him, there will come a day when this action, which the man perhaps sees as a normal and natural need, really makes her despise his lack of thought for her - and the marriage is thenceforth doomed. It might seem a small, trivial matter to the husband, but then 'women are from Venus, men are from Mars.'

When women talk, good listening skills are the key to the husband's success. In a non-extended family, the wife is dependent upon the husband for emotional support. She does not usually want to make decisions on her own, but wants her husband to agree with her, to back her up. This does not necessarily mean that she wants him to tell her what to do, but just that she needs to feel close to him and to share with him - something that usually does not bother a man at work too much.

A good husband grants her enough time, and does listen. A really good husband has worked out that she rarely comes right out with it and says what she wants or what is bothering her - she drops hints. And the irritating thing for the husband is that *she expects him to work all this out for himself*. That, for her, is a major proof that he has noticed her and taken consideration of her needs, that he loves her. When the husband cannot or will not do this, she nearly always assumes that he does *not* love her. To her, most things she wants seem such little things to ask - why can't he even give her that?

Women generally listen hard and pick up all sorts of signals and body language, to see behind the words to what people feel, and what they are thinking. They frequently know intuitively what people want, or need. This is a skill that many men do not emphasize or develop. However, on the down-side, women can become overcome with emotions over small matters, and draw sweeping, dramatic conclusions out of a shrug or a sigh, something which is exasperating and baffling to a husband.

Husbands could perhaps remember that it is highly likely that throughout her childhood his wife had a close friend, someone to whom she talked about *everything*, especially feelings, likes and dislikes, loves and tragedies. They may have 'lived' together through the turmoils and passions of heroines in books and magazines. They shared and empathised about everything, including the most intimate emotions. When childhood is left behind and the girl marries, she very frequently expects the husband to become her new 'best friend', and take on the role of 'confidant' where her old girl-friends left off. When the man proves unable to do this, she is often (perhaps unconsciously) disappointed, and feels left out and lonely.

Women often talk away to their friends, pouring everything out, not hesitating to reveal their fears and troubles. They do not expect their friends to judge them, merely to share their emotions. It may well be that in marriage a woman also has a very strong need for an empathetic listener. But she has very likely forgotten that her husband, coming back to the home after a day 'on the outside', has his own fears, worries, and need for solitude and refreshment.

Tired husbands will often ignore the petty day-to-day squabbles and upsets, assuming that if there is a *real* problem the wife will speak up. The tired wife gets upset over the fact that he is ignoring her obvious state of distress, tiredness and hints. Many husbands do not really listen to 'feelings', but to problems and how to solve them. Their reaction to her tirade is usually that she is *over-reacting* - her problems are small and very easy to solve.

And the wife explodes again. How dare he consider her problems to be small? She is doing all this, sacrificing all her life for him, slaving away in drudgery, etc. etc., for him. Irritated, the husband tends to withdraw, shut out her noise and the noise from the kids, and retreat to somewhere quiet where he can put his feet up and relax, and maybe mull over his own day's problems.

What do husbands really expect from their wives? This is another matter that really needs sorting out. They usually need to feel that the health of their families is in safe hands; they expect the wife to buy the proper food and cook proper meals, and keep them fit and well.

They expect their wives to make some effort to look nice, on their behalf. They expect wives to watch the clock and get themselves ready at appropriate times. Of course, if *they* break the rules and pop up unexpectedly, or bring people in without notice, they are asking for a nasty surprise.

They expect their wives to keep their home looking decent, welcoming and clean. Children and toys all over the place can be a major irritant. The answer is usually to have a play-room, if possible, or at least to keep a large toy-box handy where everything can be slung in quickly, out of the way.

75

They expect their wives to be pleased to see them, gentle and unharrassing, and they hope that they will not be indifferent towards them in the marital bed. In many cases, a wife's lack of enthusiasm, or sometimes frigidity, may well be due to the husband's lack of consideration and understanding. But wives should be aware that their indifference hurts the husband, and a show of distaste might kill his potency, or even cause him to be attracted to someone else.

Husbands have the right to trust their wives, and not catch them out doing things or seeing people that the wife knows the husband disapproves of.

> 'It is not lawful for a woman who believes in Allah to allow anyone into her husband's home whom he dislikes ... She should not refuse to share her husband's bed. She should not strike him. If he is more in the wrong than she, she should plead with him until he is satisfied. If he accepts her pleading, well and good, and her plea will be accepted by Allah; while if he is not reconciled to her, her plea will have reached Allah in any case.'
> (Hadith from al-Hakim.)

So once again, don't seethe with resentment because the wife is not doing what you want. Communicate! 'Darling, I used to love it when you put on a fresh dress and perfume just for me. I know the sort of day you have just had, but when you still do it, just to please me, I know that you really do still care about me.' Notice the necessary ingredients of your statement: express your hurt, acknowledge their hard work and sacrifice, state your need for love and respect - and watch the results.

Seems too much of a performance? After a little practice the skills just come naturally. They are the basic good manners (*adab*) of Islamic marriage.

8 *A Bank Balance in Heaven*

'Allah has purchased from the believers their wealth and their souls, so that Heaven might be theirs.'
(Quran, 9:111)

Marriage is *not* a bed of roses. Or, at least, if you wish to look at it in such terms, it is a bed of roses with plenty of thorns in it.

The rest of this little book is an attempt to shed some light on what makes so many marriages go wrong, so that hopefully, you who are starting out can avoid a few of the pitfalls.

The true Muslim is conscious of God at *every* moment of the day, during *every* event of life. And He is present with us not only during the grand times, when we are in the limelight, and are patted on the back when we are successful, but also in those far more frequent times when we are slogging away, coping with boredom and frustration at work or at home, and putting up with things we do not really like. He does not only see the things that are done in public, but as *al-Basir*, the All-Seeing, beholds even the tiniest things that are done behind closed doors.

Very many of those private things have to do with marriage and family. It is vitally important for believers to be realistic. It is all too easy for Muslims to read book after book extolling the wonders and virtues of Islamic marriage when the briefest of glimpses into the *actual*, private state of affairs in some homes can be horrifying.

77

Life amid the stresses of the modern world, particularly in our high-speed cities, places unprecedented strains on relationships. There is no point in being complacent and pointing to the high rate of infidelity and breakdown of non-Muslim marriages - many of the same pressures are starting to bear down on *us*. Only by remembering the Islamic virtues of compassion, selflessness and consideration, and being aware that we will be judged for every cruelty, can we steer a safe course through the stormy waters of today's social environment.

When the Blessed Prophet's wife A'isha, may God be pleased with her, was asked about the Prophet's character (*khuluq*), she responded that his character *was* the Quran. His conformity to the enlightened and wise norm of behaviour counselled by God was complete. She knew that there was no detail, however small, of his private life which would show him up in public as practising double standards. But the reality for lesser Muslims often falls far short of this ideal, if their practice of Islam is left behind with their umbrella when they step through the front door on returning home.

Muslims should realise that Allah knows not only our actions, but also our thoughts and motives. 'He knows the treason of the eyes, and what the hearts conceal' (Quran, 40:19). When people do wrong in secret, and think that they have got away with it success-fully - they are wrong! Allah has seen everything they did. Similarly, when people strive to do the right thing, and sometimes get downhearted because they think that nobody has noticed or appreciated what they did - they are also wrong.

This is an enormous responsibility for us, and also a great joy; and awareness of it can be the saving of our sanity in a bad marriage. When, sadly, some marriages begin to go wrong, it brings enormous consolation to the 'wronged party' to know that God is witness to every aspect of the situation. It can give them just the strength they need to persevere until better times.

A good marriage, to the Prophet (☸), was not just a case of a man and woman rubbing along reasonably well together. It meant a living, creative and dynamic powerhouse of goodness that would spill over and bless all who came into contact with it. A house was not just a house - it was a place of refuge, of consolation, of peace, of plenty, of provision. A bird could shelter in its eaves, or a lost traveller find shelter within its walls; a wild animal could expect to be fed at its back door, and a tired husband returning from the world outside would be welcomed at the gate.

Allah has said that husband and wife should be like 'garments' for one another (Quran 2:187). The point of a garment is to give warmth, protection and decency, and in marriage terms this includes intimacy, comfort and protection from being tempted to 'look elsewhere'. Garments are not held together by a few big knots, but by thousands of little stitches of thread. It is the continuing accumulation of small words and acts each day of our lives that 'clothe' us and reveal what we really are. Some clothing is uncomfortable and restrictive, and we are only too eager to throw it off. We need to clothe ourselves with compassion, kindness, humility, good humour and patience.

> Put on the belt of *sabr*, wind on the turban of *tawba*,
> Keep on the shirt of *zuhd*, and work hard in it!
>
> You will not travel without the sandals of fear and hope in God,
> Nor without the staff called *yaqin* or the provisions of *taqwa*
>
> (Shaykh Muhammad ibn al-Habib)

The marriage, and the home, if organised and run under the eye of Allah Almighty, should radiate certain qualities. A stranger coming to a 'submitted' home should feel this atmosphere right away - that no matter how weary the occupants, they are never too busy to be kind. When both partners feel this atmosphere, and observe the happiness and relaxation of their guests as they eat and pray with them, they should know that their marriage is on the right course.

For those people who are having difficulties with their marriages, they might like to use a little thought-technique to help them get their priorities right, and boost their morale when the road is getting rough.

The Holy Quran itself offers the following thought-technique as our aid and encouragement when beginning to get depressed, or even when sunk in the depths of despair.

'Whatever good you send forth for your souls, you will find it
with Allah; for Allah is All-Seeing of what you do.' (Quran, 2:110)

Muslims find it helpful to think of the hereafter, and Paradise, as a
kind of 'heavenly bank', and all the good things you are granted to
do as 'payments' that are going to be deposited in that bank.

'Allah does not permit the reward to be lost of those who do good;
nor do they spend anything (in charity), small or great, but that
the deed is inscribed to their credit, that Allah may requite their
deed with the best possible reward.' (Quran, 9:121)

In the Quran, Allah frequently uses this thought-picture, talking
of either your good deeds or your sins 'which your hands send on
before you' (see e.g. 2:110, 78:40, 81:14).

In other words, if you have done something wrong, then you
have indeed brought down your balance - but this is not the end of
the world. God will allow you to repay that debt; every time a
person genuinely repents of what they did wrong and makes an
effort to put it right, the 'debt' is repaid. Every time a Muslim turns
to Allah and genuinely seeks forgiveness, he or she is forgiven.
Sometimes, when the debt proves too overwhelming, He will even
excuse you the debt - because God is God, and not a human bank-
manager.

'Had it not been for the grace and mercy of Allah towards you,
you would surely have been among the lost.' (Quran, 2:64)

Allah *ta'ala* is far more generous and forgiving than human
beings. The important thing is that in trying to live the Muslim life
you keep on building up your balance of 'good payments' day by
day, in the little things you do and think as well as the big ones. That
way, when you reach the end of each day and cast your mind back
over its successes and failures, you will be able to see how you are
moving steadily forward. *This becomes vitally important if you marry
someone who does not move steadily forward with you.*

It can happen that a marriage will go wrong - as you have
perhaps seen among your friends. Of course, it usually takes two
to make an argument, and we all know that few marriages can

really break down without there being fault on both sides. But sometimes the fault really is very heavily weighted on one side or the other, and the perplexed partner who is still trying hard to keep the marriage going can become worn down and depressed. If that is happening to you, remember that 'Bank Balance in Heaven', and remember also that every time you did *not* return a bad answer, or pay back evil with evil, a little extra credit gets entered on your record.

Every individual is responsible for their own Record. When we face judgement, our 'books' will be opened, and we will see straight away what we did with our lives. When we live intimately with another person, it is all too easy to try to mix up our record with that person's, to try and mould them in the way that we believe suits us, to try to make them do what *we* want them to do. This might work; but as so many married people know to their cost, it works only rarely, and the price can be high.

You have to stand on your own, and build your own Record. If your husband or wife does something that hurts you, this bad deed or thought goes down on their record and not yours.

> 'Guard yourselves against a Day when no soul shall avail an-other, nor shall intercession be accepted for that other, nor shall compensation be taken for it, nor shall anyone be helped from outside.' (Quran, 2:48)

What is entered on your Record is how you reacted to that particular test: did you fly off the handle, or consider the truth of the matter with patience and justice? If your reaction was a successful one in the Islamic sense, then the badness of your partner is turned into merit for you - even though you have been hurt.

These words from the Holy Quran imply the correct way to conduct your Islamic marriage partnership and household:

> 'Whatever you are given is but an enjoyment for this life; while that which is with God is better and more lasting, for those who believe and put their trust in their Lord. Those who avoid the greater transgressions and shameful deeds, and who, when they are angry, still forgive; those who listen to their Lord, and do establish the Prayer, and whose affairs are settled by mutual

consultation among themselves; and who spend (in charity) out of what We bestow upon them; and those who, when an oppressive wrong is inflicted upon them, help and defend themselves. The recompense for an injury is an injury like unto it; but whoever forgives, and makes reconciliation, his reward is due from God. And God loves not those who act unjustly.' (Quran, 42:36-40)

When someone wrongs you, you may not be able to put it right, or make them a friend again - but it will be an enormous consolation to know that you have a Friend Who never changes in His concern and justice towards you, and Whose 'eye' sees all. Without this awareness, marriage can be difficult indeed.

If your main aim in marriage is to please your partner, then you could be heading for disappointment and distress, for human beings are odd creatures with fickle moods and fancies. Many disappointed husbands and wives know that no matter what they do or how hard they try, the partner is never pleased. In fact, quite often the more they do to try to earn that approval, the more it irritates the partner and the less likely they are to get it. Human nature can be that perverse.

However, if your main aim is to please Allah, then you will hopefully be able to withstand any 'bad patches', maintain your loving relationship with sympathy and patience, and remain confident that He Who sees all will understand everything that comes to pass.

9 *How to turn Sex into Sadaqa*

'Women shall have rights similar to the rights upon them; according to what is equitable and just; and men have a degree of advantage over them.'

(Quran, 2:216)

They do indeed! This passage of the Holy Quran was revealed in connection with the rights of women following a divorce, but it also has a general sense. One basic right of every person taking on a contract never to have sex other than with their own legitimate partner is that each spouse should therefore provide sexual fulfilment (*imta'*) to the other, as part of the bargain.

Now, every man knows what sexual things please him - but some men, particularly those who have not been married before and are therefore lacking experience, don't seem to know much about how to give the same pleasure to the woman; even worse, some men *do* know but they can't be bothered to make the effort. Yet *this is vital if a marriage is to succeed* and not just be a disappointing burden for the woman, and it is a vital part of one's Islamic duty. It is not acceptable for a Muslim man just to satisfy himself while ignoring his wife's needs.

Experts agree that the basic psychological need of a man is *respect*, while that of a woman is *love*. Neither respect nor love are things that can be forced - they have to be worked for, and earned.

The Prophet (ﷺ) stated that in one's sexual intimacy with one's life-partner there is *sadaqa*:

God's Messenger (ﷺ) said: 'In the sexual act of each of you there
is a *sadaqa*.' The Companions replied: 'O Messenger of God!
When one of us fulfils his sexual desire, will he be given a reward
for that?' And he said, 'Do you not think that were he to act upon
it unlawfully, he would be sinning? Likewise, if he acts upon it
lawfully he will be rewarded.' (Muslim)

This hadith only makes sense if the sexual act is raised above the
mere animal level. What is the magic ingredient that turns sex into
sadaqa, that makes it a matter of reward or punishment from Allah?
*It is by making one's sex life more than simple physical gratification; it is
by thought for pleasing Allah by unselfish care for one's partner.* A
husband that cannot understand this will never be fully respected
by his wife.

Neither spouse should ever act in a manner that would be
injurious or harmful to their conjugal life. *Nikah* is the sacred tie
between husband and wife, that sincere and devoted love without
which they cannot attain happiness and peace of mind.

'Of His signs is this: that He created for you spouses that you
might find rest in them, and He ordained between you love and
mercy.' (Quran, 30:21)

Now, every Muslim knows that a man has a right on his wife.
However, because *nikah* is a contract never to seek sexual satisfaction outside the marriage bond, Islam commands not only the
women but the men in this respect, and makes it clear that if a
husband is not aware of the urges and needs of his wife, he will be
committing a sin by depriving her of her rights.

According to all four orthodox jurists, it is incumbent upon the
husband to keep his wife happy and pleased in this respect.
Likewise, it is essential for the wife to satisfy the desire of the
husband. Neither should reject the other, unless there is some
lawful excuse.

Now, it is fairly easy for a woman to satisfy a man and make
herself available to him, even if she is not really in the mood. It is
far harder for a man to satisfy a woman if he is not in the mood, and
this is where an important aspect of male responsibility needs to be
brought to every Muslim man's attention, and stressed strongly.

Turning Sex into Sadaqa

The jurists believed that a woman's private parts needed 'protecting' (*tahsin*). What they meant was that it was important for a Muslim husband to satisfy his wife's sexual needs so that she would not be tempted to commit *zina* out of despair or frustration.

A Muslim wife is not merely a lump of flesh without emotions or feelings, just there to satisfy a man's natural urges. On the contrary, her body contains a soul no less important in God's sight than her husband's. Her heart is very tender and delicate, and crude or rough manners would hurt her feelings and drive away love. The husband would be both foolish and immoral to act in any way unpalatable to her natural temperament, and a man selfishly seeking his own satisfaction without considering that of his wife is a selfish boor.

In fact, according to a hadith:

> 'Three things are counted inadequacies in a man. Firstly, meeting someone he would like to get to know, and taking leave of him before learning his name and his family. Secondly, rebuffing the generosity that another shows to him. And thirdly, going to his wife and having intercourse with her before talking to her and gaining her intimacy, satisfying his need from her before she has satisfied her need from him.' (Daylami)

This is another of the things implied by the saying that one's wife is 'a tilth unto you' (Quran, 2:223). The imagery is that of a farmer taking care of his fields. According to Mawlana Abul-Ala Mawdudi:

> 'The farmer sows the seed in order to reap the harvest, but he does not sow it out of season or cultivate it in a manner which will injure or exhaust the soil. He is wise and considerate, and does not run riot.' (Afzalur Rahman, *Quranic Sciences*, London 1981, p.285)

Likewise, in the case of husband and wife, the husband should not just

> 'take hold of his wife and drop the seed and finish the business of procreation. The damage in this case could sometimes be irreparable, because the woman, unlike a farm, is very sensitive and has

85

emotions, feelings and strong passions which need full satisfaction and attention in a proper and appropriate manner.' (Afzalur Rahman, p.286.)

If this is not taken into consideration, and the wife is not properly prepared to start lovemaking, or is unsatisfied when it is finished, there could be many psychological and physiological complications leading to frigidity and other abnormalities. Indeed, many husbands eventually become disappointed with their wives, believing them to be frigid or unable to respond to their activities (unlike the sirens on the film or TV screen), and they wonder what is wrong with them. A possible explanation will follow in a moment.

Allah created male and female from a single soul in order that man might live with her in serenity (Quran, 7:189), and not in unhappiness, frustration and strife. If your marriage is frankly awful, then you must ask yourself how such a desperate and tragic scenario could be regarded by anyone as 'half the Faith'.

According to a hadith:

> 'Not one of you should fall upon his wife like an animal; but let there first be a messenger between you.' 'And what is that messenger?' they asked, and he replied: 'Kisses and words.'
> (Daylami)

These 'kisses and words' do not just include foreplay once intimacy has commenced. To set the right mood, little signals should begin well in advance, so that the wife has a clue as to what is coming, and is pleasantly expectant, and also has adequate time to make herself clean, attractive and ready.

As regards intimacy itself, all men know that they cannot achieve sexual fulfilment if they are not aroused. They should also realise that it is actually harmful and painful for the female organs to be used for sex without proper preparation. In simple biological terms, the woman's private parts need a kind of natural lubrication before the sexual act takes place. For this, Allah has created special glands, known to modern doctors as the Bartholin glands, which provide the necessary 'oils'.

It is still possible to read old-fashioned advice to husbands that a desirable wife should be 'dry' - which is remarkable ignorance and makes one really grieve for the poor wives of such inconsiderate men. Just as no-one would dream of trying to run an engine without the correct lubricating fluids, it is the same, through the creative will of Allah, with the parts of the female body designed for sexual intimacy. A husband should know how to stimulate the production of these 'oils' in his wife, or at the very least allow her to use some artificial 'oils'. This lack of knowledge or consideration is where so many marital problems frequently arise.

As Imam al-Ghazali says: 'Sex should begin with gentle words and kissing', and Imam al-Zabidi adds: 'This should include not only the cheeks and lips; and then he should caress the breasts and nipples, and every part of her body.' (Zabidi, *Ithaf al-Sada al-Muttaqin*, V, 372.) Most men will not need telling this; but it should be remembered that failure to observe this Islamic practice is to neglect or deny the way Allah has created women.

Insulting a wife with bad marital manners

Firstly, a husband must overcome his shyness enough to actually look at his wife, and pay attention to her. If he cannot bring himself to follow this *sunna*, it is an insult to her, and extremely hurtful. Personal intimacy is a minefield of opportunities to hurt each other - glancing at the watch, a yawn at the wrong moment, appearing bored, and so on. A husband's duty is to convince his wife that he *does* love her - and this can only be done by word (constantly repeated word, I might add - such is the irritating nature of women!), and by looking and touching.

Many people believe that the expression in the eyes reveals much of the human soul. Certainly the lover's gaze is a most endearing and treasured thing. Many wives yearn for that gaze of love, even after they have been married for years.

If you cannot bring yourself to look at her while paying attention to her, she can only interpret this as a sign that you do not really love her. And even though it may be irritating to you, and seem quite superfluous, most women are deeply moved when a man actually tells her that he loves her.

Sex is clean!

A modest upbringing is part of good character. The Prophet (ﷺ) himself said: 'Modesty brings nothing but good'. (Bukhari and Muslim.) But another, also important part of Islamic teaching says that all of Allah's creation is beautiful and pure, particularly when it is part of the body of human beings, who are designed as His deputies upon the earth. In some religions, people traditionally believed that the woman's private parts are in some way unclean, or dirty, or even evil. In the Islamic view this is nonsense - they are simply part of the way Allah created women. To criticise or to dislike this is to criticise our Maker himself, who out of His kindness gave women this equipment and opportunity for the physical expression of love and union.

> 'If the woman is *halal* for him, he may look at all parts of her body.'
> (Zabidi, *Ithaf al-Sada al-Muttaqin*, V, 331)

> 'A husband is permitted to look at the private parts of his wife.'
> (Khurashi, *Sharh Mukhtasar Khalil*, III, 4)

There is a very relevant ayah in the Quran which says: 'If you take a dislike to them, it may be that you dislike something through which Allah is bringing about much good.' (4:19)

Anyone who finds his wife's sexual equipment distasteful is insulting her Creator, and ignoring His plan and wise reasons.

Sex is not dirty if the couple are not dirty, either physically or in harbouring 'dirty' thoughts of self-gratification and the abuse of the spouse. This should not be a problem for Muslims, who have such clear guidance on personal hygiene that their private parts are washed several times a day, which is not the case in any other religion. But in addition to the usual Muslim hygiene, if a man does feel that his wife is dirty, it is a simple matter to exert a husband's right as the boss and give her the order to wash. At the same time, the man has the duty to *make sure he is clean himself!*

Some women feel exactly the same qualms about the cleanliness of a man's private parts as he might do for hers. Don't forget that a man actually does urinate and spend his seed from the same orifice, which is not true for the woman! Her urine comes from quite a different place than the one intended for physical intimacy.

It is perfectly possible for a husband to touch a woman's vagina and clitoris, and not touch the part from which urine comes at all.

The Blessed Prophet actually recommended regularly removing the pubic hairs - a tricky operation for the woman, but preferable for a clean and stimulating attitude to sexual coupling.

If, after taking a shower before sex, and perhaps using a favourite perfume, the man still thinks the woman is dirty or unclean, then he is being ignorant, and unrighteously critical of Allah's creation and intentions, and is neglecting his own duty.

What about those wrinkles?

A good Muslim does not waste time complaining to the Creator about the physical 'bag of tricks' he or she has been given for this lifetime. It is a complete waste of time for a man as thin as a stick to wish that he were a rugby player; or someone with blue eyes wishing they had brown; or someone with ginger hair trying to dye it another colour; or a short person trying desperately to be tall; or an ageing person wishing to be young again, and so on. Although we can sometimes make marginal improvements with great effort; basically we are as we are, warts and all.

The amazing thing is that it is not the appearance of our physical bodies that makes our partner love us. Certainly it is true that human beings probably cannot help an instant reaction when they look at another human being for the first time. But even in very materialistic societies, people's looks are often not the reason why they fall in love. They need have little to do with a happy marriage. 'A man who marries a woman for her wealth and beauty will be deprived of that wealth and beauty; while the man who marries her for her religion shall receive from God her wealth and beauty too.' (Hadith in Tabarani.)

Being unduly concerned about any aspect of one's looks can have a very detrimental effect on a marriage, especially if the person's desire to change something or other in their body overwhelms them and becomes their chief concern. It is the duty of all of us to make the best of what we have; but it is a subtle form of *shirk* to live in an attitude of complaint to our Creator for what we have been given.

O friend, friend! Be neither anguished nor distressed,
Surrender to God's Decrees, and you will be praised and rewarded.
Be content with what He has ordained and disposed,
Do not despise the decree of He Who is the Lord of the High Throne.
(Imam al-Haddad)

Nevertheless, loving people realise that those they love are often very sensitive about certain things. Having stated that husbands should pay their wives the compliment of actually looking at them, particularly during intimate moments, it also needs to be stated that many women appreciate the cover of darkness, and only feel comfortable being intimate in the dark, when all their 'warts and all' become invisible. Women are sensitive things - signs of ageing or physical 'imperfections', little defects like double-chins, rolls of unwanted spare tyre round the belly, all sorts of spots and blemishes, these are just as upsetting to a woman as flapping ears, pimples, the inability to grow hair, being too thin or too short are to the male ego. Sometimes the darkness is kind to us, and loosens up our inhibitions.

How can I make my woman happy and satisfied?

It is important for men to realise that women are *not* all the same, but are actually individual living beings. They do not have automatic response mechanisms, but their responses are subtle and are triggered by all sorts of things.

Contrary to a very common male myth, the love of a woman for a man has nothing to do with the size or shape of his private parts. Most women do not find the common male fixation with his size at all endearing, and might even be frightened by something they thought was too much for them (even though we all know that babies, some with heads the size of a grapefruit, have to come out of that same channel!). In any case, unless the erect member is less than three inches long it will still be perfectly capable of bringing her to orgasm, since the deeper parts of the vagina are not very sensitive.

As regards the man's body, unexpected things like the shape of his arm, the fineness of his hands, the way he stands or walks, his hips, the strength of his legs, the nape of his neck, the fine hairs on his cheek - all these things stir a woman's longing response far more than contemplation of his actual sexual equipment.

Basically, what attracts a woman most is a man's *manliness*. It may even be his awkward shyness, or his cussed determination, or his ability to take command. Certainly, if the man is a good leader and dominant partner, the most wonderful thing about marriage with him will be his ability to 'descend from his lofty heights' and actually do and say things for no other reason than to please his wife.

The little gift, the bunch of flowers, is a prime example. The woman doesn't actually care tuppence for the flowers - what gives her such wonderful pleasure is the thought that her man has actually taken the time and trouble to think about her. That is certainly one thing that would make her love him, so long as it is done in a Muslim way, and not as a bribe or other sweetener. 'Give gifts to each other, and you will love each other.' (Bukhari.)

There is a lovely story of the Blessed Prophet listening to eleven women. They all complained about their husbands, but the eleventh one, Umm Zar'a, said: 'I have no words enough to praise my husband. He has covered my ears with ornaments, and fed me so well that my lean and thin arms have become plump. In short, he has provided me with everything to keep me happy, and I am happy. I am very lucky ... I talk to him freely and frankly, but he never objects. I sleep comfortably until the morning, and I eat delicious food.' Then the Blessed Prophet said to A'isha: 'I am like Abu Zar'a for you!'

The importance of kindness to your woman

A person embarking on a journey across strange territory will be well-advised to consult a map. Similarly, it is a good idea for anyone embarking on marriage for the first time to have a rough idea of what to do and how long to do it for. For a Muslim man contracting *nikah*, this is a duty. A man getting married can probably already imagine what pleases him, and what it is necessary for him to do or experience, and for how long, for him to achieve satisfaction and a good, restful night's sleep to follow.

He already knows that if he is turned on by something, and then is forced to 'cool it down', 'turn it off', and not be fulfilled, this takes a considerable effort of will, and is not a pleasant business at all.

Imagine a hungry cat being shown a plateful of food. Once the food is seen and smelt, the cat goes crazy to have it. You hold the cat back, but the instant you let go, it leaps upon the food. It is perfectly natural for it to do so. Can you imagine how unjust it would be to a female cat if the male was always allowed to finish the meal and eat just as much as he liked, while the female always had the plate snatched away from her after she had just taken a bite at it?

Nobody who kept a pet cat would ever dream of making this distinction between their male and female animals. They would see and agree straight away that it was gross cruelty, and totally in opposition to the will of Allah, Who has counselled kindness and consideration to all creatures.

But sometimes men do this to their women, and it is a gross dereliction of their duty. Sometimes human beings develop one particular blindness - they forget that they also have a biological nature, male and female, and that all their needs and urges and intuitions are implanted in them by their dear Lord, the Benevolent Creator.

As regards sexual fulfilment, if a man knows that he is not going to be able to achieve it, he is likely to make a considerable effort not to let his body become aroused in the first place, or if it is he will probably have worked out some means acceptable to himself of satisfying the urge aroused, even though he may feel unhappy about this.

Allah created the sexual urge in us, and it is probably the strongest of all the urges He created. He intended it to be used, and He intended us to form a happy marriage bond with a life-partner; so there is nothing wrong whatsoever in thinking through ways of achieving the best in marital happiness.

A happy and fulfilled night life leads to better sleep, contentment, a better work routine during the day, confidence, and a whole range of other benefits. It should be obvious that a happy sex life is as much a part of Islam as prayers or fasting!

Turning Sex into Sadaqa

How to help a wife achieve satisfaction, peace and love

It is all too easy for a man to be aroused and to charge into sexual intimacy, and, because of his excitement, for it all to be over in a matter of moments. If this is the case, the woman is likely to be frustrated and unhappy, even if she has not the courage or is too polite or shy to say so.

If you are a man, and have just read the preceding paragraph, and it suddenly occurs to you that this is indeed what *you* do, but of course it doesn't apply to your wife - she is perfectly happy - then you would be well advised to stop and scrutinise the evidence. How often does she smile and show her contentment? How often does she hurry to please you in all sorts of little ways? How ungrudgingly does she do the boring and unpleasant chores of family life on your behalf?

Given a good, attentive lover, she will do the most menial of tasks for him, cheerfully! But if he lacks attention, she will gradually be worn down by disappointment and resentment, and the whole pleasure of family life intended by God in His mercy towards us will wither away.

Some men mistakenly believe that they cannot help being the way they are. In fact, they may have thought it a compliment to their wives that they are able to rouse themselves and fulfil their urges so speedily. This is nonsense. If you read any medical manual on the subject, you will discover that if a male reaches climax in less than three minutes after entering his woman, this is counted as 'premature ejaculation' and is thought of as something that one has to make an effort to cure.

On the medical level, there are some useful counter-measures for this common problem. Take a look, for instance, at the Islamic herbal remedies listed in Chishti's *The Traditional Healer*, pages 276 (for impotence), and 278 (for premature ejaculation).

Another useful way of solving the problem is to raise the significance of your intimacy by setting aside more time for it, rather than leaving it until last thing at night when you are exhausted. It is worth remembering that the traditional time for sex in many Muslim societies is not the night, but the afternoon siesta. This is not so easy if you are at work on a 9 to 5 job! But perhaps, occasionally, you could go to bed an hour earlier. It is highly insulting to a wife if the only attention she ever gets is an abrupt announcement of her husband's urges, perhaps after he has sat up late watching TV, after which he rolls into bed to get the whole business over with as quickly as possible before he drops off to sleep

Similarly, there is no justification for using one's religious devotions as an excuse to deprive a loving partner. According to Abu Sa'd, the Prophet (ﷺ) once rebuked the wife of Safwan ibn al-Mu'attal for being over-pious to the detriment of her marriage. She used to read two long suras during her night prayer, keeping her husband waiting; and she fasted frequently without his permission, which made her tired and prevented any opportunity for sex during the day (sexual activity being forbidden while fasting). The Blessed Prophet ruled in favour of the husband, recommending that she limit her recitation to one sura, and only fasted with her husband's permission. Similarly, when the Prophet heard that an ascetic Companion, Abdallah ibn 'Amr, was in the habit of praying all night and fasting all day, he told him to moderate his devotions, pointing out that 'Your eye has a right over you, your guests have a right over you, and your wife has a right over you.' (Bukhari.)

This hadith should be taken seriously. Many Muslim wives in nuclear families know only too well the long hours of loneliness while their husbands are away at the mosque, and how frequently they dawdle with their friends (even if the last prayer is very late), and sometimes fail to come to bed until the wife is already asleep, or is so tired that she is no longer interested!

The Blessed Prophet's own practice was not to remain in the mosque or with others after the last prayer of the day, but to leave the mosque and return home. It is a *Sunna* to sleep quite early, and to rise early as well.

If some of the above reads like a comment on your own attitude or activities, then you would do well to examine your conscience! Nobody is suggesting that a normal marriage has to be a constant round of physical gymnastics at every moment of the day - merely that the legitimate needs of *both* partners must be taken into consideration.

A good Muslim woman will do her best to see that her man is happy and content. The good Muslim man must know that he has exactly the same duty towards his wife.

Sometimes he fails in this duty simply because he is a selfish man and a poor Muslim (even though he may find time for his five prayers). Sometimes, tragically, Muslim men can fail out of simple ignorance of what their responsibilities entail, and make themselves suffer as well as their wives, quite needlessly. This is not what Allah intended for either of them in their marriage - and with a little effort and knowledge, it could so easily be put right. This is what this final part of my book is all about.

If a man is consistently refusing to provide the answer to his wife's *du'a* for his kind attention he must realise that he will find some awkward questions to answer when he eventually faces Judgement, and the books are opened to reveal all - no matter how shaming! He may have thought of himself as the 'best of Muslims', without realising the truth of the words of the Prophet: 'the best of you are those who are kindest to their wives and families.' Imagine the shock, at the end of a pious lifetime of prayer and charity, of discovering that you had actually been guilty of cruelty towards your wife all those years, and were now called to account for it!

Thankfully, every day is a new day, and it is never too late to make a fresh start and put things right. 'A Muslim's repentance is accepted until he gives the death-rattle.' (Hadith in al-Hakim, *Mustadrak*.)

10 *Sexual Problems*

'The more a woman feels desire, the more she will be desired.'
(Ibn Qutayba, *Uyun al-Akhbar*)

'May Allah grant glory and eternal salvation to those who know how to stroke a soft cheek in an accomplished manner, to give a just accolade to a slender waist, and to enter the sweetest *farj* with a befitting skill!'
(Imam al-Suyuti, *Kitab al-Idah fi ilm al-nikah*)

There is a widespread belief that the sexual problems of society at large do not exist in the Muslim community - or are at least uncommon. Sadly, the dislocation many Muslim families have experienced over the past generation or so means that this rosy assessment is often misplaced.

One such problem is that of husbands who are baffled that sex, which seems very enjoyable to them, does not seem in the least enjoyable to their wives. They begin to wonder what is wrong with them. Has it been their misfortune to marry a frigid woman? Or is it that she simply doesn't care for him at all? It all seems so enigmatic - but then women are a mystery, aren't they?

Poor men! The answer often lies in their own ignorance of women's sexuality - and the answers to their mystified questions are really so easy! Those sensual decadent American women on the films do not enjoy sex any more or less than the most chaste of Islamic village maidens - God made their equipment more or less the same. It is what the man learns to do with it that counts. Husbands - it is basically up to you.

A Muslim man who has the intention to create a happy marriage should start, as with all things, in prayer, submission to God, and deep thought - not to work out his own will, but to discover the will of his Lord.

In fact, the Blessed Prophet recommended that one should always begin sexual intimacy in an atmosphere of prayer. He said:

> 'If, when you approach your spouse, you say: "In the name of God! O Lord God, protect me from the devil, and protect from the devil that which You grant to us", then, if a child is conceived, the devil shall not harm it.' (Bukhari and Muslim.)

> (The meaning of 'not harming it' in this hadith is that the devil shall not overcome it ... no scholar has held that it is to be taken at face value to mean that such a child will never experience any harm, whisperings or temptations from the devil. (Qadi Iyad, *Sharh Sahih Muslim*.))

Imam Ghazali further suggests that the lovers should begin with *Bismillah* and Surat al-Ikhlas as a way of increasing the blessing of the sex act. And when approaching orgasm, they should quietly say: '*Al-hamdu li'Llah alladhi khalaqa min al-ma'i basharan.*' ('Praised be Allah Who has created human beings out of water.')

Doctors get asked so often how often one should 'perform' per week. This can't be answered. Some people would enjoy intimacy three times a day or more, while others are quite content with once a fortnight, or even less! It all depends how long your sexual activity takes, how much pleasure and satisfaction it gives, and so forth. (It is interesting to note that the caliph Umar reckoned that a woman had the *right* to sex at least once every four days, while Imam Abu Talib al-Makki added that 'if he knows that she needs more, he is obliged to comply.' (Zabidi, *Ithaf*, V, 373.))

However, it has to be said candidly that one reason why men so often feel threatened and dismayed by female sexual hunger and capacity is *not* that their women are over-sexed at all.

97

Whenever women are accused of this, you should suspect male selfishness and/or ignorance! All too often when these men do mate they only gratify themselves and, having seen to their own needs, do not even attempt to bring the woman to climax. Therefore the woman remains 'hungry' and unfulfilled, and looks for further opportunity when the man is sated - and thus she gets accused of being over-sexed. This is a pitiful but all too common injustice. In any case, the level of an individual's sexual appetite, rather like brainpower, is not the choice of the individual but is largely a matter granted by Allah at His direction.

As is well known, the early Muslims regarded sexual prowess and the ability to satisfy a woman as being an essential part of manhood. The niece of A'isha, a scholarly and beautiful woman called A'isha bint Talha, once married the pious Umar ibn Ubaydillah. On their wedding night he made love to her no fewer than seven times, so that when morning came, she told him: 'You are a perfect Muslim in every way, even in this!'

Such stories are common in our literature. But the only true answer to the question of 'how often' for a dedicated Muslim is *whatever is right for you as a couple*. It is *not* 'whatever is right just for *you*'! You *must* consider your wife's needs and feelings, just as you would wish her to consider yours.

In the West, this sort of thing is often investigated before commitment to marriage, the idea being that finding a 'good' sexual partner before marriage will reduce the possibility of disappointment later. But figures released in 1993 showed that people who had cohabited before marriage were 60% more likely to get divorced than those who had not. In fact, the divorce rate in secular countries proves that the idea of 'testing the waters' does not work at all. In any case, Muslims cannot approve of this because our Lord has not sanctioned physical intimacy before marriage. Muslim partners endeavour to get their needs understood and sorted out as soon as they are able to do so, *after* marriage.

But talking is sometimes so difficult. Shy women will very rarely say what they really feel on the subject, either because of natural modesty, or because they fear that their husbands will interpret their words as criticism. They do not want to upset or to hurt their spouses, or make them feel small, or a failure.

Sexual Problems

The price the woman sometimes has to pay for her loving concern for her husband's feelings is a lifetime of 'the cat seeing the meal, but having it snatched away each time she starts to eat.'

No man who is aware of this, and carries on ignoring it, can be considered a complete and good Muslim. In fact, it is a form of extreme and damaging cruelty.

Every man should appreciate that despite some common myths, *it rarely takes less than 15 to 30 minutes of specific sexual activity* to arouse a woman to a level where her physical satisfaction is in sight.

Do not despair - this does not mean that a man has to 'perform' for that length of time: although some women might think it would be very nice if he could, others would be horrified at the thought. *There are other things that a man has to do.*

According to Imam al-Ghazali:

> 'When he has come to his orgasm (*inzal*), he should wait for his wife until she comes to her orgasm likewise; for her climax may well come slowly. If he arouses her desire, and then sits back from her, this will hurt her, and any disparity in their orgasms will certainly produce a sense of estrangement. A simultaneous orgasm will be the most delightful for her, especially since her husband will be distracted by his own orgasm from her, and she will not therefore be afflicted by shyness.' (*Ihya*, II, 46.)

Selfish modern lovers would do well to consider the words of this great Imam, written nine hundred years ago!

But suppose a man cannot help rushing to his climax so quickly that his wife gets no pleasure from his intimacy at all? He should not just think about his problem, but take some decisive action. One rather obvious solution (which nevertheless does not always occur to many men) might be to come to climax quickly, as usual, then after arousing his wife for twenty minutes or so while he rests, try again! This would need the wife's consent, for the first quick climax might be painful for her.

He should not worry that he may not be able to achieve full satisfaction for himself the second time. He may surprise himself and have no bother at all, or it may be that the unfamiliarity of the sequence prevents him from achieving full satisfaction at all this time - and he may feel ashamed of himself or think that he has

99

failed. This is, incidentally, very often the reason why a man who is not hampered by actual tiredness or lack of opportunity nevertheless does not attempt anything further than his own instant pleasure. He fears that he may fail; and does not realise that his wife will not think of his attempt in the same terms!

Never mind if he 'fails' or 'feels frustrated' this time around - remember his poor wife probably ended up frustrated every time he approached her, if he always ejaculated just when she was warming up! Just think about why he is attempting it - it is not in order to satisfy himself, but just to offer a little more satisfaction to her.

Another suggestion that often helps is that the couple overcome their shyness enough for the wife to practise the technique of gently squeezing his penis just below its head, thereby stopping a climax and prolonging the act of intercourse. The same effect will be achieved if the angle of the penis is altered by gently pushing it down towards his legs, almost to the point where it becomes uncomfortable. The husband's excitement can also be reduced by mental effort: he could try thinking about something completely unconnected with sex. Skilled husbands develop the ability to delay their orgasm simply by willpower, by telling themselves firmly that it is too early. In fact, according to Imam al-Zabidi: 'Some strong men control themselves so perfectly that they have their orgasms only when they wish. What can one say about them, other than "Allah gives what He will to whom He will!"' (Zabidi, *Ithaf*, V, 373.) Needless to say, this rare achievement requires plenty of practice. A life with plenty of spiritual effort and prayer will help to provide the essential discipline here.

There is a physiological solution which can be used in conjunction with these techniques. This can be found in traditional Islamic medicine, which prescribes a range of natural remedies to increase female sexual enjoyment and thus speed up the onset of orgasm. (See Chishti's *Traditional Healer*, 285-93.)

The most usual popular alternative is for the husband to bring his wife to climax by caressing. This needs sensitivity and judgement, for often the wife really is not in the mood, or is in pain, or is too tired for sex, in which case her husband's normal quick sexual act will be sufficient.

Sexual Problems

Some inexperienced husbands do not realise that many women cannot reach climax at all unless the man caresses them. The man has to be able to touch his wife intimately *with his hand*. For some women, this is the *only* way they can reach fulfilment. The husband (who usually is very well aware that the woman does have a clitoris, even if he is not quite sure what to do with it!) has to realise that just to press down on it with some part of his anatomy, like his foot curled around her, or pressure from his knee, is not enough.

Most men usually understand quickly the techniques of stimulating the female breasts, and especially the nipples, with kisses or with their fingers, an act which is an effective but supplementary means of helping the wife towards *inzal*. Imagine trying to caress her breast with a foot or knee! Exactly the same applies to the clitoris. It is a much more sensitive area, should be treated with great care, and if it is caressed properly (a matter worked out by practice and communication with the wife) it will usually bring the woman to readiness, or to climax, very quickly. Men need to remember, of course, that if they are caressing their wives in the wrong way or in the wrong place, it will hurt rather than cause them pleasure. So care, sensitivity, communication and practice are vital here.

While some people may at first dislike using their fingers, it should be emphasized that there is *no Islamic objection* to it. Imam Abu Hanifa was once asked about a husband's touching the private parts of his wife, and vice versa, and he replied: 'There is nothing wrong with that, and I hope that their reward will be great.' (Zabidi, *Ithaf*, V, 331.)

Once this is mastered, it is also worth knowing that most women also have a third very sensitive area (the 'G-spot') inside the vagina - not deep inside, but a few centimetres in on the upper wall. This is one reason why the size of a man's penis is not particularly important for a woman - very few experience much sensation in the depths of their vaginas, near the womb. The G-spot always gives great pleasure if caressed with the fingers, or if the penis is angled in the right direction. When the wife shuffles about during sex, this may be because she is trying to get you into the right position for this.

To find the G-spot, insert the forefinger into the vagina and rest the fingertip on the front wall, about two-thirds of the way along the vagina towards the cervix. You should feel a small configuration of muscles that are able to resist firm but gentle pressure.

Finding the G-spot can greatly enhance the woman's sexual pleasure and enable her to experience much quicker and more intense orgasms.

This could be one reason why the Prophet (ﷺ) defended a man's right to 'come to his tilth' from behind, for that position often gives the woman far more pleasure than face-to-face. But there are many other positions which have been recommended by the ulema. These include the 'scissors', where the husband and wife are at an angle to each other. Some people enjoy the 'woman on top' position, where she either faces the husband's face and shoulders, or faces away from him. Any position that enables the husband to touch his wife's pleasure zone with his fingers at the same time as he is within her will bring her far more satisfaction - and face-to-face with the woman beneath is the one position where such caressing becomes very difficult.

It should be obvious that people's shapes should be taken into account in finding the best position. If a man is thin, he probably cannot even imagine the problems faced by his stouter fellow. The man has to fit himself comfortably into the shape of his wife's hips in order to connect well. If he is a large-boned man, or inclined to be fat, the straightforward face-to-face position is not going to be at all satisfactory for either of them, and could actually be painful for the woman. They should try some of the other ways of coming together.

Bear in mind, too, that if the wife is shy about her breasts, she is going to be very shy indeed about her even more private areas, and for a man to overcome his feelings and then gently deal with her shyness is all part of being an intelligent and successful Muslim husband.

As we pointed out earlier, it is obvious that the husband should not leap into action with full force and expect her instant capitulation if not ecstasy, as is so frequently depicted in films. X-rated movies, although they show complete nudity and the sex act in shocking detail, do not actually show real or realistic sex. That would be boring - remember it takes the average woman more than fifteen minutes to get anywhere. Remember that the actresses are not 'real-life'; they are not portraying the realities of married life - they are 'prostitutes of the eye', whose business is fantasy and not reality.

Women are extremely sensitive and tender, and the husband will only hurt her and be pushed off, or at best be 'tolerated' and not 'enjoyed', if he is rough and abusive. Gently does it! Start in first gear, not fourth. If a husband goes slowly and with reverence for the Muslim woman he loves, and then increases his fervour, he will soon be gratified to see her happy response - and what a difference this will make to the marriage!

Some men go through their entire married lives being gross and clumsy, and never discover that making love is quite a talent. As a result, they have never enjoyed the experience of making love to a fully aroused woman. When a woman is fully aroused, she cannot control the exciting movements, known as *qabd*, made in her vagina. Some men never find this out - a terrible and needless tragedy.

We saw above that many women need specific caressing by hand to their erogenous zones to continue right through the entire act of lovemaking if they are to achieve *inzal*. This may involve some minor sacrifice and discomfort for the husband, if he cannot work himself around to some satisfactory position, and especially if he is being overwhelmed by his own climax. Don't worry! No woman actually expects her man constantly to be on the look-out for her own gratification all the time, for that would be just as selfish as the man *never* thinking about it. This is something that will be worked out gradually between the couple.

A Muslim husband will make it his business to find out what she likes, and if possible, to carry on doing it right through his own climax. The most beautiful and exciting sexual relationship comes when a couple have practiced and know each other so well that they can reach climax at the same time, even though this takes considerable skill. If for some reason this cannot be managed, then the man should carry on doing what she likes afterwards, even after his *inzal* is complete, until she has caught up. More gratifying for him in many ways is the technique of bringing her to climax first, before he himself lets go. We have already seen the importance which Imam al-Ghazali attached to the simultaneous orgasm, and that 'he should not satisfy his need from her before she has fulfilled her need from him'. But whatever happens, once the husband has reached his climax he should not just leap away and charge off to the bathroom leaving her in abject despair, hypertension and shock!

To reach climax together is something that takes considerable practice and expertise, and some couples never achieve it properly in a lifetime together. However, Imam al-Ghazali was raising a very important point when he mentioned the wife's shyness if the husband was satisfying her after achieving his own *inzal*: it is only natural for the man immediately to lose all interest in sex and want to go off to sleep, so the poor wife feels that in order to claim her Islamic right she has to irritate him, and make him impatient with her. Once disturbing thoughts like these enter her head, it only delays the orgasm even more, and perhaps prevents it altogether, thereby producing real psychological harm. Hence the very sad but common situation of wives who are too kind or tactful towards their husbands' feelings actually faking their orgasms, and then becoming so frustrated that they indulge in lonely masturbation behind his back. However hard she may try, disappointment and resentment will be hard to avoid - and these are two of the most powerful marriage-killers in the devil's arsenal.

Most married women know only too well how difficult and embarrassing it can be to try to request physical satisfaction from a tired husband who has just satisfied himself, and who then instantly turns over and drops off to sleep, perhaps blithely and ignorantly assuming that what he has just done *has* satisfied her. ('We've had sex, haven't we? Aren't you *ever* satisfied?') Many wives find themselves totally unable to get their men to understand the true state of affairs.

Many men do not seem to realise that very few wives can achieve any physical satisfaction from the simple animal act of placing the penis in the vagina alone. Allah simply did not make them that way. It may be enough for a man, but it is almost never enough for a woman. It should be obvious that if Allah had simply intended that that should sum up the sex act, He would not have created the rest of the female equipment. On its own, the vagina almost never brings satisfaction, unless the man can hold out for a very long time indeed - which is a rare accomplishment.

This means that if a man is not strong enough to conquer his shyness about touching his wife, his modesty, far from being a virtue, actually becomes a direct cause of marital cruelty.

Another way of increasing the wife's frustration is for the couple to lose contact, or for the man to 'come out' and be spent outside his wife's body, or for the man to seek his satisfaction without placing his penis in the wife's vagina at all. This might be one way of managing contraception, but it is extremely frustrating for the woman, and is another destroyer of marital enjoyment and harmony. The Blessed Prophet said it should only be done with the wife's permission.

If a man does deliberately ejaculate outside a woman's vagina (some men enjoy this), he should realise that this is not full intercourse, and may not grant the wife any satisfaction at all - even though she has accepted it and is eager to please him! The purpose of *Nikah* is lost if the spouses fail to satisfy in each other the natural hungers that Allah has created.

The legal aspect of 'coitus interruptus' (withdrawal before ejaculation) in the revealed law is fairly complex. The Hanbali school reckons that a man does not need his wife's permission, on the assumption that she does not have the automatic right to his ejaculation; nevertheless, Ibn Qudama al-Maqdisi, the most 'hardline' of this school, still maintains that obtaining her permission is preferable for the sake of amity. The Hanafis reckon that the woman has to give permission, except when times are very hard so that any children conceived are likely to be in for a miserable existence, in which case the husband is allowed to use contraception without her permission. The Maliki school actually allows the wife to demand and receive monetary compensation as the price of her permission! The Shafi'is hold that the woman's consent may be sought as a precondition for the marriage contract, after which she cannot complain.

Finally, good *adab* is also necessary after lovemaking. This is something that is particularly important for the husband to remember, if he wishes to have a happy wife. Remember that his basic need is for respect, while hers is for love. Just as a man would hate to be laughed at for sexual inadequacy, so a woman hates to be 'used' and then set aside without a word of love.

The correct Islamic manners for a husband are to lie with his arms round his wife for some moments, after checking her happiness, telling her that he loves her, and in his heart thanking Allah for his happiness and good fortune.

Conclusion

Once sex has become a chore and a duty, the marriage is well on its way to being dead. If the man's efforts actually cause the woman pain or distaste, she will soon avoid any intimacy at all, and will use any excuse to get out of it. Headaches, weak heart, rheumatism - you name it, she'll have it.

In fact, a real sexual relationship is so good for you it would help to heal all these conditions, since it is good healthy activity that raises the heart rate and stimulates the lungs, and takes the mind off disturbing problems and brings spiritual wholeness, serenity and contentment.

The considerate Muslim man soon learns how to make his wife happy, and in doing so, refuses to get anxious and overwrought about his own performance. A good Muslim wife will never despise a husband for his physical equipment or lack of expertise, so long as he is loving and considerate towards her. And if they married as virgins, there will be no unfavourable comparisons for either of them to make!

If a good Muslim marriage is to be *sadaqa* for the spouses and pleasing in the eyes of God, it is no use one partner seething with frustration and then finally cracking up. Both of them should try to find gentle ways of supplying 'feedback' to the other - not to be interpreted as criticism, dissatisfaction or hostility (which is what it becomes if left to ferment for too long), but as the only way to learn and grow together, as sanctioned and willed for us by Allah.

May Allah forgive this author for raising topics that are sensitive and private, and discussing them in a way that some might think incorrect and distasteful. But we know that many Muslims nowadays are asking about these matters, and it is the *Sunna* to make useful knowledge known, whatever it might be.

Allah *ta'ala* decreed that creation should be set up in pairs complementing each other in harmony, and wished only happiness and peace for us. Therefore, we should all make it our *jihad* to create happy and fulfilled marriages, in the sight of Him in Whose 'hand' lie our souls. May everything we do be pleasing to Him, and may He bless us and bring us to fulfilment, serenity and completion. *Amin.*

11 *A Short A to Z of Marriage*

'The quest for knowledge is every Muslim's duty.'
(Hadith from Ibn Maja)

'You will not have faith until you love one another.'
(Hadith from Muslim)

ABANDONMENT. A major sin. Imam al-Ghazali records: 'It is related that if a man runs away from his family, Allah will not accept his prayer or his fasting until he returns home.'

ABORTION. The Prophet (ﷺ) believed that every conceived child had a right to life, and there are strong Quranic ayats against the killing of children. 'Do not slay your children for fear of poverty. We provide for you and for them.' (6:151)

Every human being has a living soul, and should be loved, respected, and have his or her proper place in a family. Muslim jurists are of the unanimous view that after the foetus has been given a soul by Allah, it is forbidden to kill it. An unborn child has legal rights, depending whether it was formed and showing signs of independent life. If it was, and if someone hurt a pregnant woman and she miscarried, full *diya* (blood compensation) has to be paid, just as for an adult person. A foetus can also inherit. The *janaza* prayer is performed for a 'formed' foetus, and it is given a name. If the foetus is not 'formed', *janaza* is prohibited.

108

The majority of jurists are of the opinion that the soul does not enter the body of the unborn baby until the time it is 'ensouled' (*nafh al-ruh*), which is in the sixteenth week of pregnancy; and if an abortion is absolutely necessary, it has to be performed before that time. The Hanafis permit abortion until the end of the fourth month. Others, particularly the Maliki scholars, feel that the matter of when the soul enters the foetus is unproven, and therefore prohibit abortion absolutely.

The Hanafis grant women the right to an abortion even without the man's permission, but urge that this not be done without genuine and pressing reasons.

After 'ensoulment', abortion is only allowed if the pregnancy will endanger the mother's life, the principle being that the real life of the mother takes precedence over the potential life of the unborn child.

A casual attitude to abortion has developed in a few countries, where it is often used routinely whenever contraception fails, but it is now increasingly realised that many women who have abortions in order to solve one problem end up with psychological problems later on as the result of the guilt and sadness of destroying their unborn child.

ABSTINENCE. Sometimes a couple decide to live without sex for a period of time. This is not generally advisable in a marriage, because it can lead to a range of inhibitions and problems. If both parties wish to rest from sex, then that is their business. Both partners have to agree, of course, as the *Shari'a* forbids either to renounce sex without the other's permission. There is a danger, however, that marital relations may not start up again, and the man and wife may be attracted to others. Islam is alert to the need to prevent adultery, and therefore sees abstinence as encouraging a temptation that is unnecessary.

'Allah desires ease for you, and He does not desire hardship for you.' (Quran, 2:185)

There is a hadith of Salman al-Farisi to Abu'l-Darda', whose wife had begun to neglect herself because she was so depressed by her husband's lack of care for her: 'Allah has rights over you, and so do your wife and children. So try to fulfil all these rights. The fulfilment of one duty should not cause the negligence of others.' When the Prophet (ﷺ) was informed about this, he said that Salman was right. (Bukhari.)

See also 'Celibacy'.

AGE. It is generally best if the husband is older than his bride, because women seem to mature more quickly, and also because he will be better able to support her financially.

As far as the sex drive goes, this diminishes far less quickly with age than is commonly imagined. Sexual activity will continue well into the sixties and even seventies, provided that the couple have developed an active and varied sex life from early marriage, and have taken steps to avoid getting bored.

AIDS. This terrible disease is transmitted sexually, or through the sharing of hypodermic needles. Most victims are homosexuals, but it is now spreading among the heterosexual population as well, and some unfortunate children are being born with it. The only protection is to go into your marriage without previous illicit sexual contact, and to remain faithful to your partner.

The Blessed Prophet remarked:

> 'Never does immorality appear among a people to the extent that they make it public, but that there shall appear among them plagues and agonies unknown to their forefathers.'
> (Malik, *Muwatta'*)

It is hardly necessary to remark that men and women who have come to (or come back to) Islam from a promiscuous background should have an AIDS test before they get married.

For some palliatives for AIDS in Islamic medicine, see Chishti, *The Traditional Healer*, 283-4.

ANAL INTERCOURSE. Some people find this gratifying, although most women do not, and are grateful that the Prophet (ﷺ) spoke out strongly against it. Abu Hurayra reported that he said:

'Do not approach women from the anus.' (Tirmidhi.)

'Allah will not look at the face of he who has committed sodomy with his wife.' (Ibn Maja.)

110

This practice still seems to be quite common in some societies, and is a very traumatic thing for a woman to be forced to submit to. It has been used as a method of contraception, of not spoiling a girl's virginity, or as a novel method of intercourse in a tighter 'channel' than the vagina. According to the Hanbali scholar Ibn al-Qayyim:

'It is the right of the wife that her husband should have natural sexual relations with her. By committing sodomy he deprives her of her right, and also fails to satisfy her sexual desire ... She was not created for this dirty act. Hence all those who avoid the natural course and indulge in unnatural means have ignored the wisdom of Allah and His *Shari'a*.' (Ibn al-Qayyim, *Zad al-Ma'ad*)

Incidentally, it should be made clear than when the Prophet (ﷺ) sanctioned 'intercourse from behind', he did not mean anal intercourse, but vaginal intercourse from behind. But there is nothing wrong with enjoying the areas nearby. Imam Zabidi says: 'To enjoy the back-side without entering the rectum is permissible, because with that exception, all parts of a woman's body may be enjoyed by the husband.' (*Ithaf al-Sada al-Muttaqin*, V, 331.)

ARBITRATION (*tahkim*). In cases where the spouses seem unable to resolve a dispute, it is useful to put it to arbitration. The Holy Quran explains how this is to be done: 'If you fear a split between the two of them, then appoint an arbiter from his family and an arbiter from her family. If they wish for reconciliation, then Allah will reconcile them. For Allah was ever Knowing, Aware.' (4:35)

ARRANGED MARRIAGE. A good thing if all parties are happy with the match. It is not permissible in *Shari'a* for a woman to be married against her will.

A'isha, may Allah be pleased with her, once asked the Prophet (ﷺ) whether a family who wished to marry off a young girl should ask her permission, and he said: 'Yes, her permission should be sought.' (Muslim.)

Imam Nawawi:

'The woman has a right over herself concerning marriage, and her guardian has a right over her concerning marriage; but her right takes precedence over his. If he wishes to marry her to someone of a proper background, and she refuses, then she cannot be compelled; while if she wishes to marry someone who has a proper background, and her guardian refuses, he will be compelled to submit to her wishes; and if he persists in his refusal, the *qadi* is authorised to give her away in marriage in his stead.'

(*Sharh Sahih Muslim*, IX, 204)

BEATING. See under 'Corporal Punishment'.

BODY ODOURS. Underarms, underpants, and feet. Keep them sweet. See 'Cleanliness'.

BREASTS. An important erogenous zone (see Chapter 10). If they get sore, rub in 'Masse' cream, available at any chemists.

BREATH. Some people have an awful problem here, especially smokers and *pan* chewers - and they may not realise it. First thing in the morning is another dangerous time for bad breath. All married Muslims have a duty to make themselves as palatable as possible for their spouses. Newlyweds might like to keep a packet of mints under the pillow, to be sucked on waking. Keep a *miswak* handy, and use it regularly. Smokers, especially pipe smokers, should do something about their breath before they attempt to have sex. Islam strongly condemns smoking anyway, and getting married would be a good opportunity to give it up!

CELIBACY. The *Sunna* of the Prophet (ﷺ) was marriage, and he regarded total celibacy as unnatural and against the will of Allah. Anas ibn Malik recorded the case of a man who decided that all troubles were caused by marriage, and so instead of marrying he would pass his life in prayer. When this came to the attention of the Prophet (ﷺ), he said: 'By Allah, I keep *nafl* (optional) fasts, but I also discontinue them; I pray at night, but I also sleep; I also marry women - and this is my *sunna*. Whoever shuns my *sunna* is not of me.' (Bukhari.)

'O young people! Whoever among you is capable of sexual intercourse should marry, for that is more modest for the gaze and

112

safer for the private parts; and whoever cannot, should fast, for that is a form of castration.' (Muslim)

A'isha recorded that he said: '*Nikah* (marriage) is my *sunna*, and he who shuns my *sunna* is not of me.' (Muslim)

'Anyone who refuses to marry is shirking his farm-work, wasting the seed, and leaving idle the appropriate tools created by God; he sins against the purpose of creation and the wisdom visible in the evidence of natural structure. The man who refuses to marry has severed a chain of being, a previously unbroken chain linking his own existence to that of Adam.' (al-Ghazali)

A bachelor once asked Imam al-Ghazali: 'Which should I choose: marriage, or total devotion to God?' 'Both', he replied.

It is related that after his death, the pious bachelor Bishr al-Hafi appeared to someone in a dream, and was asked: 'How has God treated you?' 'I have been given a high rank in the Garden of Paradise,' he said, 'and was allowed to look upon the stations of the Prophets; yet I never attained to the ranks of the married.' When asked what had become of Abu Nasr al-Tammar, he replied: 'He has been raised seventy degrees above me.' People were surprised, and asked how this could be, and he answered: 'He earned that by his patience with his little daughters and his family burdens.'

Celibacy of the unmarried is to be solved by marrying someone suitable as soon as possible, in the light of one's financial circumstances, while widows and divorced people should try to remarry.

CHILDREN. These should always be welcomed and wanted. It is irresponsible to bring into the world children who will be hurt because they are not wanted. This is one of the things you have to think most carefully about even before you get married, because it is all too easy to get pregnant very quickly, even on the wedding night, and your families may well put pressure on both of you to do this. See 'Contraception'; and also the texts by Silma Buckley and Dr. Alia Schleifer mentioned at the end of this book.

CIRCUMCISION (*khitan*). According to some *madhhabs*, this is not completely obligatory for adult male converts, but it is nevertheless a very strong *sunna*. An uncircumcised penis quickly accumulates smelly material under the foreskin, and medical studies have indicated a connection between failure to circumcise and cancer of this organ.

'Female circumcision' of the type practiced by some people in Somalia, Egypt and some other African countries is a mutilation forbidden by Islam.

CLEANLINESS. This is one of the basic aspects of Islam, and has been likened to half the faith. (Hadith in Ibn Hanbal.) It is certainly vital to marriage, as we saw in Chapter 10. The Blessed Prophet recommended ten things as being part of the *fitra*:

> 'Cutting the hair close on the lips, letting the beard grow, using the *miswak* for the teeth, cleaning out the nose, paring the nails, washing out the base of the fingers, removal of the hair in the armpits and pubic areas, washing the affected parts after a call of nature, and the rinsing of the mouth.' (Muslim.)

Some people need reminding of the obvious point of *adab* that not all of these cleansing activities should be done in public. People who have shaved off a large amount of hair in the bath or shower should remember that it can clog the drains. The Prophet's preferred method of disposal of hair-cuttings and nail-parings was burning or burial, since these are part of the human body, and should not be discarded with ordinary filth and rubbish. See also 'Washing' below.

COIL. See I.U.D.

COITUS INTERRUPTUS. Some people use *azl* - 'coitus interruptus' (the male withdrawing from the female just short of climax) as a form of birth control. It is very unreliable. The Blessed Prophet allowed it as a method of contraception, but only with the wife's permission.

Some men practised it when their wives were suckling children, so as not to risk impregnating them again to the detriment of the baby. Others used to practise it when their wives were pregnant, superstitiously fearing to harm the unborn child (in fact, there is no evidence that sex during pregnancy is dangerous). Usama narrated that a man once came to the Prophet (ﷺ) and said: 'O

Messenger of God, I withdraw from my wife during sexual inter-course.' The Prophet (ﷺ) asked why, and he said that it was that he might not harm the child. The Prophet (ﷺ) replied: 'If there was any truth about harming the child, the people of Persia and Byzan-tium would suffer the same harm.' (Muslim.)

The Caliph Umar said it should never be done without the wife's permission; and the scholars hold that this applies to all forms of contraception.

CONDITIONS (*shurut*). When a man marries a woman he takes upon himself certain conditions as duties, of which the *Shari'a* specifically mentions kindness, financial maintenance, clothing, sex and accommodation, all in accordance with the woman's background and normal expectations. If he fails to comply, he is sinning and the wife can take him to an Islamic judge to force him to mend his ways. If she lays down additional conditions for her marriage before the actual ceremony takes place, he must honour these also, as long as they do not invalidate any Islamic principle. According to the *madhhab* of Imam Ahmad ibn Hanbal, the bride can make it a legal condition of the marriage that the husband will not take a second wife. (Nawawi, *Sharh Sahih Muslim*, IX, 202.)

'The condition most deserving to be honoured is that through which you make private parts *halal* for you.' (Hadith in Muslim.)

CONDOM. If you are using these as your only method of contra-ception, remember that they easily split, burst or slip off, and there is quite a high rate of accidents. If you really don't wish to conceive, use a spermicide as well, or some other *halal* contraceptive.

CONTRACEPTION. This is important if you do not want twenty children! There are numerous methods, and you should consult your doctor for advice. Islam is not against any method of contra-ception that prevents the conception of a child, but it *is* against destroying a foetus once it has life. Choose a method that suits both partners, not just one of you. Contraception should always be done after consultation.

If the wife chooses to go 'on the Pill', remember that there are sometimes side-effects, and that it is not always advisable to take a drug over a long period of time. Taking the Pill is often recom-

115

mended for new wives because it is relatively safe and foolproof, but doctors often recommend taking a break from it after a couple of years.

Some varieties of the Pill are not permissible in the view of those *madhhabs* that regard all abortion as sinful, as they cause the fertilised egg to be dislodged and lost, which is a kind of early abortion. 'Morning-after' pills are of this type, killing the embryo after fertilization has taken place.

Taking the body temperature regularly can indicate the times when ovulation is most likely; and avoiding these times is the most natural method of contraception. However this 'rhythm' method is notoriously unreliable - and because of its favour among Catholics it has been nicknamed 'Vatican Roulette'! Remember, too, that most women feel most sexual desire at the very time when they are ovulating, so other means must be taken if they are to have a satisfactory sex life.

CONTRACT. An Islamically-valid marriage requires the fulfilment of five obligatory conditions: (1) the consent of the guardian (or in his absence, or unjust refusal, the *qadi*); (2) the consent of the man and the woman; (3) the agreed-upon dower (*mahr*); (4) two Muslim witnesses of good character (*shahiday adl*); (5) an 'offer and immediate acceptance' (*ijab wa-qubul*) using the word 'marriage' or 'wedding'. Practices which are *sunna* but not obligatory are: (1) the engagement proposal (*khitba*) made earlier to the guardian or in his presence; (2) the religious speech (*khutba*) before the marriage; (3) the bride and groom should see each other and learn about each other before consent is given; (4) friends and relations should attend the ceremony; (5) the couple should intend 'upholding the Sunna, preserving modesty and seeking offspring'; (6) the ceremony should ideally take place in the local mosque and during the month of Shawwal.

CORPORAL PUNISHMENT. The Prophet (ﷺ) did not forbid a man from giving instructions to his wife, as long as these were in accordance with Islam, or from giving his wife some form of physical discipline - even though he himself never struck any of his wives. However, this did not mean that a husband was allowed to

116

beat his wife for things like burning the dinner, or forgetting something she should have done, or simply because he was in a foul mood!

There is one Quranic verse that grants husbands permission, but it states that this is only in cases where they genuinely fear *nushuz* ('rebellion', which in this context means treating the husband with arrogance and refusing the marital bed as a permanent principle, not just the odd occasion when the woman might have been ill).

> 'Men are the protectors and maintainers of women, through that in which Allah has given one more than the other, and because they support them from their means. Therefore the righteous women are devoutly obedient, and guard in absence what Allah would have them guard. As to those women on whose part you fear rebellion, (first) admonish them, (next) refuse to share their beds, (and last) beat them; but if they return to obedience then do not seek against them any (further) means.' (Quran, 4:34)

The Prophet referred to this verse in his Final Sermon. He said:

> 'Hear me well! Treat your women kindly, for they resemble prisoners in your hands ... if they are guilty of flagrant misbehaviour, you may remove them from your beds, or beat them, but do not inflict upon them any severe punishment! Then, if they obey you, do not seek against them any (further) means. Hear me well! You have your rights over your wives, and they have their rights over you!'

The idea of punching or beating up a woman was totally repugnant to the Blessed Prophet, and belonged to the attitude towards women shown in the time of *Jahiliya*, or of societies where the consumption of alcohol was widespread. The hadiths tell us that he laughingly suggested that if a husband was obliged to spank his wife, he should use a *miswak*, the soft stick which Muslims use to clean the teeth (Tabari, Baghawi) or even a handkerchief (Razi).

A balance has to be struck between being a responsible male caring for a partner's earthly life and eternal fate (in trying to make her do the right thing), and allowing her the freedom to be herself - for in the end, her fate will be of her own making. It is obvious that when this permission was abused by violent men, the Prophet was

117

very quick to listen to the complaints of the wives and rebuke the husbands.

Ibn Sa'd, for instance, comments that 'the Prophet (ﷺ) had always persisted in his opposition to the beating of women. And men came to him to complain about their women; then he gave them permission, but said: "I cannot bear to see a quick-tempered man beat his wife in a fit of anger."' (Ibn Sa'd.)

The Prophet (ﷺ) also said: 'How can any one of you beat his wife as he might beat a camel, and then expect to embrace her at night?' (Bukhari and Muslim.)

According to other hadiths, he appears to have forbidden the beating of women completely: 'Do not beat Allah's handmaidens!' (Abu Daud, Nasa'i, Ibn Maja, al-Hakim.)

Put together, all these sources suggest that beating, if it has to be done at all, should be a last resort to punish a wife for some major sin, such as adultery. It is the final manifestation of the husband's authority, not the first; a deterrent aimed at holding the marriage together.

DAUGHTERS. In some Muslim cultures influenced by non-Islamic traditions, these are welcomed less than sons. This attitude is condemned by Allah. Islam criticises the pre-Islamic Arabs by saying:

> 'When one of them receives the good news of [the birth of] a female, his face remains darkened, and he is angry within. He hides himself from the people because of the evil of that of which he has been given good news: Shall he keep her in contempt, or bury her beneath the earth? Evil indeed is their judgement.' (Qur'an 16:58)

> 'A man who has three daughters, and who maintains them and treats them well until God makes them independent of him, to him God will grant the Garden irrevocably, irrevocably, unless he commits an act which is unforgivable.' (Hadith from Khara'iti)

> 'A man should not be too overjoyed at getting a boy, or unduly sad when he is given a girl, for he cannot know which of them will turn out to be the greater blessing for him. How many fathers of sons wish they had had none at all, or girls instead! In fact, girls

give more peace, and the reward they bring from God is more
bountiful.' (Al-Ghazali)

DOMINANT MALES IN BED. Most women rather like their men
to be dominant, so long as they know they will not be forced to do
anything they would not wish to do. Many wives enjoy quite
'rough' sexplay, being 'forced' (in a pretence situation) to comply
with a husband's wishes - it can be quite flattering! Some even
enjoy being spanked if 'naughty'. However, remember that other
women would not like this at all. It is not safe to assume that when
your wife says 'No' she really means 'Yes'. Every man has the right
to be the leading partner in his marriage, and there are few women
who really appreciate 'soft' men, although they may never care to
admit the fact! However, men should always be very careful to
observe where to draw the line, and never hurt their wives. There
is always a difference between fun and cruelty, and Islam has no
place for torture and abuse.

DOWRY. In the Subcontinent, the practice of giving dowries to the
bridegroom or his family is on the increase among Muslims, but
this habit is hardly known elsewhere in the Islamic world, and is
almost certainly a borrowing from Hinduism. According to the
Sharia, it is the man who has to give a wedding-gift, not the other
way around, the idea being to make him take the marriage seriously, and to provide her with some financial security. The practice
of the Companions was to hand this *mahr* over at the time of the
marriage itself. See also 'Weddings' below.

DRY PARTS. A frequent cause of painful intercourse in women,
and hence of marital stress. It can be caused by nervousness, illness,
or inadequate foreplay. Lubricants such as 'KY jelly' can be bought
over the counter in any chemists.

EGO (*nafs*). This is the biggest problem of all! Nothing in Islam is
easy until the lower and selfish desires of the *nafs* are under control.
Happiness and fulfilment in marriage come about through making
sacrifices for the sake of spouse and children; and such sacrifices
will be painful and perhaps even impossible if one's own ego
regularly wins its battles against mind (*aql*) and spirit (*ruh*).

119

There are many ways of controlling and weakening the *nafs*. The first is observing its activities, and cutting down on things it is strongly attached to, such as laziness, suspicion, or even certain types of food or TV programmes. Fasting can be a real help here. It is also important at the end of every day to think back over one's actions, and consider how to rectify obvious faults and acts of selfishness. Saying each prayer at the beginning of its time, and regularly reciting the Holy Quran and any *wird* or *wazifa* you may have, will also help to grind down the ego, and replace its darkness with light and ease in the heart.

'And as for him who fears the standing before his Lord, and forbids his *nafs* its whim, assuredly the Garden shall be his place of refuge.' (79:40)

FANTASIES. Almost everyone has these. Sexual fantasies in dreams are not sinful, just the workings of an active imagination. No-one could be held to blame for the content of their dreams, since this is out of their control. They are only harmful if they become a major part of your waking life so that they damage your partner, or turn into an obsession that makes a normal relationship difficult.

A good Muslim will obviously try to live in reality, rather than in a fantasy. He or she will try to avoid consciously fantasising about something that is forbidden in Islam, even though thinking about doing something but not doing it is not considered a sin.

Fantasies can sometimes prove useful as mental stimulants when a marriage is growing stale. But it is not always a good idea to reveal your fantasies to your partner - they could well have a good laugh at your expense, or, alternatively, feel threatened by them if they think that the spouse is getting bored or disappointed.

FATHERHOOD. This usually comes as a shock the first time round. Couples are often unprepared for the sheer exhaustion, if they are not in an extended family situation which can ease the strain. Babies cry a lot, need feeding at night, and so on. Things are never the same again - you cannot put the clock back. To make matters worse, babies often come along just at the time when the husband is trying hard to get on at work. Although these days there are various aids to help busy mothers (like disposable nappies), the decline of old-fashioned family life means that there is often no doting granny or aunt to help look after baby, and the stress for mothers can seem overwhelming. Many new mothers feel tired and sometimes depressed as a result, just when everyone is expecting them to be bouncing around with enthusiasm. Actual physical help and a lot of sympathy and love are the Muslim husband's duty. Also, men have to realise that the experience of childbirth is so total for a woman that her feelings for him may be pushed into the background, and although it is foolish for a man to feel jealous of his own child, this often happens. A Muslim woman tries to ensure that her husband is not neglected, and that he shares her love for the baby. It is very important that the husband picks up and loves the child, helps to nurse it when sick, and generally relates to it. A wife should not be expected to recommence intercourse with her husband for at least six weeks, and even then, if they are both too tired, it is important to reestablish a loving and private relationship that is consoling and tender.

FOOT MASSAGE. This is sheer delight for some people, and torture for others. It can also be highly beneficial to the health - get a book on massage or reflexology, or go on a course.

FRIGIDITY. Women appear frigid when they do not wish to make love to their husbands. This is not normally because they *are* frigid, but because they are unhappy about their spouse for some reason. It could be because the husband always waits until the wife is too tired, or fast asleep; or because he is not very clean, or his breath smells, or he does not bother to prepare his wife for lovemaking, or because sex has become painful to the wife, or something of a chore. It is the duty of a Muslim husband to be alert to the needs of his wife, and act with sensitivity. (Remember, when your wife won't speak to you, she is trying to tell you something!) If men could talk to their wives, and listen to what they say, so much female frigidity could probably be defeated once and for all! See Chapter 10, and Chishti, *The Traditional Healer*, 285-93.

GENEROSITY. The Holy Quran warns frequently against niggardliness. Good Muslims 'prefer others over themselves, though theirs be the greater need.' (59:9) Remember your spouse regularly, and offer gifts and surprises. A Muslim wife will always be on the lookout for little ways to treat her husband - husbands should try to return the compliment. Some men will go to any lengths to impress wealthy male friends, and yet cannot bring themselves to buy their wives a box of sweets!

> 'Whatever you spend for the pleasure of Allah, you will be rewarded for it. You will be rewarded even for that morsel which you put in the mouth of your wife.' (Bukhari and Muslim)

> 'The dinar you have spent in the way of Allah (is the one used) to liberate a slave, to help the poor, or on your wife and children; while the one that fetches the highest reward is the one you spend on your wife and children.' (Muslim)

> 'Give the worker his wage before his sweat dries!' (Muslim)

G-SPOT. See page 101.

HEAD MASSAGE. Another delightful way of expressing your love and care.

HOMOSEXUALITY. This is not allowed in any revealed religion. We should recognise, however, that a few people do have a mental inclination towards the same sex, and the evidence is growing that this is often due to a defect in the chromosomes. Every human being is a mixture of male and female traits, and sometimes a person is born with an inner balance unsuited to his or her physical characteristics. Nowadays, when the distinction between male and female character is being increasingly blurred in the population at large, homosexuality is becoming more socially acceptable to the secular mind. This is no justification, of course, for committing what is the most unnatural of all human acts; but Muslims have to recognise that a person struggling for self-control deserves approval. The increasing recognition of this tendency as a genetic rather than a purely moral problem holds out hope of medical treatment, as technology advances; and the day may not be far off when all human beings can benefit from the delights and responsibilities of parenthood.

122

'What - of all creatures do you come unto the males and leave the spouses which your Lord created for you? Assuredly, you are a people who transgress the limits.' (Quran, 26:165-6)

'Do you approach men in lust rather than women? You are a people that are ignorant.' (Quran, 27:54-5)

HOUSEWIFE. Never say that a woman is 'only' a housewife. This infuriates every woman. It is a massive, demanding job, sometimes without a break for sixteen hours a day, and there is no retirement age! It requires intelligence, forethought, compassion and skill, and should never be thought of as inferior to so-called 'real' jobs outside the home. In fact, it is usually more difficult! If a man is lucky enough to have a housewife, he should appreciate her as one of life's greatest treasures. The *sunna* of the Blessed Prophet was to help his wives cheerfully: he helped with the less pleasant 'chores', and lived in appreciation and respect for his wives. (See pages 22 and 56.)

IMPOTENCE. For the penis to become erect the blood-vessels inside it must be relaxed to allow blood to flow in. If they cannot relax, either because of tension or disease, erection cannot occur. Nearly all men experience this at some time or other, and it is recognised as a particular problem in stressful modern societies. It may be that a man is too tired, or anxious, or his mind is full of something, or he may simply be ill. It is the duty of a Muslim wife to be very patient, and not act in a way that would upset the husband or make him feel like a failure, since that would make the problem far worse. Wives should not stress their husbands by making demands of them at these times, but should show that they still appreciate and respect them, perhaps by some tenderness that does not lead to full intercourse. In most cases, the husband will soon pick up again. A good Muslim wife has the duty to ensure that her husband's diet is adequate and that he is generally in good health. She will also encourage him to take regular exercise. For some Islamic herbal remedies see Chishti, *The Traditional Healer*, 276-8.

Husbands with recurrent difficulties of this sort should pluck up the courage to see a doctor, as the cause is often a disease of the arteries, and there are new 'conventional' treatments available such as Prostaglandin E1 which are frequently very effective.

I.U.D. (Inter-uterine device, or 'coil'). This is a plastic loop inserted into the uterus by a doctor, and left in place for long periods of time. It can sometimes be expelled or be painful, and it needs renewing every two years. Not usually recommended until after bearing the first child, and not recommended in Islam because it allows conception to take place but then prevents the embryo from embedding itself in the wall of the uterus.

JANABA. The state between sexual emission or penetration, and *ghusl*. It is permissible to sleep, eat, and do most things in this condition, but not to touch the Quran, or to mention sacred words and phrases more than is absolutely necessary.

KISSING. A few cultures do not seem to include kissing in their sexual repertoire, but most people find it a vital part of lovemaking, especially in the preliminary stages. The Blessed Prophet once rebuked a man who claimed he had never kissed his children; and the case of a man who never kisses his wife will presumably be similar! There are many different kinds of kissing, and they all require a clean mouth and teeth, and fresh breath (remember your Miswak!). Muslims should not inflict kisses on their spouses which are distasteful to them, and both should realise that there are skills to be learned. The kind of behaviour seen in films may be distasteful to them, and sexual kissing and petting (as opposed to the kiss of the relative as part of a greeting) should not be done in public.

LOOSE TALK. Never speak about your intimate life to another person, unless you are seeking medical help. Loose chatter about intimate things is extremely damaging, and you will never know to whom these secrets will be passed on, or when they will return again to embarrass you.

> 'On the Day of Judgement the lowest person in the sight of God will be the man who is intimate with his wife and then broadcast her secrets.' (Hadith in Muslim)

An A to Z of Marriage

'A man should never discuss sexual matters with any of his wife's relatives.' (Imam al-Nawawi, *Sharh al-Arba'in*)

MALE EGO. A husband should recall that he is not making love to his own ego, but to his wife. He has an unconscious need to impress himself, but he will be more impressive if he listens to his wife, and works with her as a team.

MAKING UP. Ending a row can be the sweetest moment in a marriage.

> 'If a woman, on her husband's being displeased, says to him that she will not sleep unless he is pacified and her hand is in his, she is deserving of Paradise.' (Hadith in Tabarani)

MASOCHISM. There are many women and men, especially, it seems, in Anglo-Saxon and Protestant cultures, who cannot achieve orgasm without the fantasy of beating or being beaten. (See 'The Role of Muslim Women in Society', Afzalur Rahman, Seerah Foundation, 1986, pp.416ff, quoting Dr Norman Haire in the *Encyclopedia of Sexual Knowledge*, p.315.) Where this is only 'token' in nature, rather than a real desire to be tortured and abused (something which requires spiritual and medical attention), it can on rare occasions enhance a marriage, when the partner is kind and considerate as regards the fantasies of the other.

MASSAGE (*tadlik*). This is a wonderful part of marriage, very important in the traditional Islamic world, and all couples should buy a book or go on a course to learn it. Obviously it should be a two-way act of love. It is not right for the husband to accept his wife's labours on his behalf, and not be willing to return the compliment. See 'Head massage', 'Foot massage', and 'Treading.'

MASTURBATION (*istimna'*). Although the Prophet (ﷺ) advised fasting to develop will-power and weaken the sex drive of unmarried people, this is a common (albeit very private) practice among young people who have not yet married. It seems to be particularly common in societies where marriage is left late. Most Muslim scholars permit it in the absence of a legitimate partner to satisfy one's desires. For instance, Imam Ibn Hanbal and Ibn Hazm allow it for those who fear that without a sexual outlet they might otherwise commit adultery or fornication, such as those financially unable to marry, prisoners, travellers, and others (both men and women) without access to a legitimate partner.

Masturbation should not be necessary once a person is married, but in some cases it persists. On occasion, where birth control is not available, men can get into the habit of some form of masturbation instead of intercourse, so that their wives do not get pregnant. Many men do not realise that if they choose deliberately to come to climax outside the wife's vagina, then this is really a form of masturbation. The Prophet (ﷺ) recommended that this be done only with the wife's permission, because it will leave the wife open to possible temptation to *zina* if her husband is not satisfying her. And some women get so little satisfaction from their husbands that they secretly carry out these rather sad practices rather than tell them and hurt their feelings or risk rejection.

MEN UNUSED TO WOMEN. If a man has not had to live with sisters, he will often be quite taken aback by female 'trappings', such as tights hanging up in the bathroom, or girl's underwear on the radiators. The most important woman in his life has been his mother, and he may expect his wife to have the same habits and views, opinions on going out to work, looking after husbands, and so on - in which case living with a modern young woman may come as a shock! Worse, if his mother spoiled him, he may be completely untrained, and may even have treated his mother rather like a servant, and now expects his new wife to endlessly run round after him picking things up. A good Muslim man takes on marriage as a new form of living, and should be willing to be sympathetic, to be helpful, and to adjust to the new situation. A Muslim wife recognises that in some ways men nowadays always remain boys, but it is her duty to make him take responsibility for himself and his children - she is not his slave!

'Make things easy for people, and do not make them hard; cheer people up and do not rebuff them.' (Hadith from Muslim.)

MENSTRUATION. See 'Periods'.

MODESTY (*haya'*). Most Muslim women are extremely modest - the Prophet (peace be upon him) said that 'modesty brings nothing but good' - and so do not like to be looked at when nude. Have respect for your wife's feelings, and allow her to retain some clothing or put out the lights if she feels happier that way. Otherwise, she may be very inhibited and unhappy. Similarly, some Muslim men prefer to retain some clothing when in the bedroom. There is nothing whatsoever wrong with this. Others enjoy complete nudity, which is acceptable also. The scholars hold that is permissible to look at the private parts of one's spouse. (See page 88 above for more details.)

> 'When anyone from among you wishes to have sexual inter-course with his wife, he should pull a cover over him, and they should not be naked like two donkeys.' (A weak hadith in Ibn Maja)

NAGGING. The idea is to wear down the partner by continually going on about something. It rarely works, is never attractive in either partner, and can push a marriage onto the rocks because of one partner's tireless campaign to change the character of the other rather than loving them for what they are. The Prophet (peace be upon him) disliked nags and gossips, and those with caustic tongues - no matter how religious they were.

> A man said: 'O Messenger of Allah, such-and-such a woman has a reputation for praying to an enormous extent, fasting and giving charity, but she harms her neighbours with her tongue.' He replied: 'She is of the people of Hell.' Then the man mentioned another woman who didn't fast or pray much, but who 'gives a piece of curd as sadaqa, and does not harm her neighbours with her tongue.' He replied, 'She is of the people of Paradise.' (Ibn Hanbal)

And remember that your spouse is your nearest 'neighbour'!

MOTHER. Men need to remember that a wife is not a mother. A young woman just starting out is not likely to have all the social skills of the older woman. A good Muslim mother will have sat the bride down and given her a few clues and tips as to things that will please her husband - but it is not her place to 'push in' or become interfering and a cause of stress or rivalry. The Muslim man, while honouring his mother, should not make his wife resent her, but should help her to acquire the skills so that she will in her turn learn the art of motherhood herself.

> 'O Messenger of God, to whom should I be loyal and good?' 'Your mother.' 'And then whom?' 'Your mother.' 'And then whom?' 'Your mother.' 'And then whom?' 'Your father.' (Tirmidhi)

OVULATION. From the onset of puberty (usually when a girl is about 12 or 13) the female releases one 'ovum' (*buwayda*, egg-cell) every month, and this continues until she is between 45 and 50 years of age (the 'menopause'). If the ovum is not fertilised by male sperm, the ovum and the lining of the uterus come away as blood (a 'period'). Most women ovulate every 28 days, but some have cycles as short as 21 days. See 'Periods'.

PERIODS (*hayd*). New husbands often haven't got a clue about these. The matter should be explained to them, or they may get worried and upset, and not know how to sympathise with the wife's symptoms. Husbands need to know that the wife may bleed from 3 to 7 days in a period of time roughly corresponding to the lunar month, and that she may well be extra tired and weepy at these times. Women frequently suffer from PMT (pre-menstrual tension) for anything up to a week before their period starts. If they do, they are likely to be bad-tempered, depressed, illogical, and suffer from psychological disorders, and some are even at extra risk from things as serious as driving accidents, or moral disorders such as temptation to theft, etc. Sympathy is the best thing to offer - and make sure the wife has had medical advice. It is quite normal for doctors to recommend cutting down on salt (to limit water retention and bloating).

Some women also experience considerable physical pain at this time, and become sick and faint. Do not suffer in silence - go to a doctor.

A woman is not 'dirty' during her period time unless she does not wash; the Prophet (ﷺ) recommended keeping up close contact with a menstruating wife, so that she did not feel hurt or rejected.

His advice was to make sure she was well-covered between the navel and the knees, and to caress and enjoy her without penetration.

> A man questioned Allah's Messenger (ﷺ) , saying: 'What is permitted to me of my wife when she is menstruating?' He said: 'Let her wrap her waist-wrapper round herself tightly, and then what is above that is for you.' (Malik, *Muwatta'*)

> On one occasion A'isha was sleeping with him in one garment, when suddenly she jumped up and left his side. The Messenger (ﷺ) said to her: 'What is the matter? Are you losing blood?' She said, 'Yes.' He said, 'Wrap your waist-wrapper tightly about you, and come back to your sleeping-place.' (Malik, *Muwatta'*)

POLYGAMY (ta'addud al-zawjat). Islam did not institute plural marriages, but acknowledged that they are sometimes of value, restricting the maximum number of wives to four:

> 'Marry women that seem good to you, two or three or four; but if you fear that you shall not be able to deal justly (between them), then only one.' (Quran, 4:3)

Polygamy can be a useful and caring way of resolving serious difficulties. It can be a solution, for instance, when a wife is suffering from a disease such as paralysis which prevents the husband fulfilling his needs, and consumes his time with caring for her. It can help in situations where she is of unsound mind, or has a bad character that cannot be reformed. And in social circumstances where women greatly outnumber men, as after a war, it can save thousands of women from being left 'on the shelf' - half a husband being preferable to none at all.

A few, however, believe that Allah has in fact forbidden plural marriages, on the grounds that it is impossible for a man to deal justly between co-wives.

'You will not be able to deal equally between wives, however much you may wish to.' (Quran, 4:129.)

Nonetheless, the fact that polygamy was part of the Prophet's *sunna* makes it impossible that he could have adopted this interpretation himself. But he counselled strict fairness in expenditure, allowances and time-sharing:

> 'When a man has two wives and he does not observe equality and deals unfairly with them, he will come before the Throne of Justice with only half of his body.'
> (Hadith in Tirmidhi and Abu Daud)

The *Sharia* tells us that the women should receive equal financial maintenance and be accommodated in separate but equal homes. Obviously, it is not permissible for more than one woman to be in one bed at any time.

A happy polygamous relationship, perhaps a *ménage a trois* in which one woman looks after the home while the other is free to work without feeling guilty, can be a source of great strength to the women. But given human nature, the pitfalls are many and varied, and no-one should enter upon this kind of marriage unless there is a compelling moral rather than a selfish reason for it, and the full and intelligent consent of *all* parties has been obtained. Anything else is likely to end in disaster.

POWER GAMES. No Muslim, male or female, is permitted to use or withhold sex to get their own way - either as a bribe, or for barter.

> 'Gentleness adorns everything, and its absence leaves everything tainted.' (Muslim)

> 'If a man invites his wife to sleep with him and she refuses to come to him, then the angels send their curses on her until morning.' (Bukhari)

See 'Refusing Sex' below.

PRAYER (*salat*). It is important to a close relationship to pray together as much as possible. One purpose of the *salat* is to bring people closer together through spiritual and physical proximity, and this can be especially therapeutic in marriage. It also has the effect of attracting angels to the house.

PREMATURE EJACULATION. See pages 92-3, 100 above.

PREPARATION. Sex without foreplay, known in the West as a 'quickie', may be suitable on some occasions, but is likely to make the wife frustrated and unhappy if practised a lot. See pages 85-6, 99.

PRIVACY. It is fatal to have sex interrupted by phone calls or children. Take the phone off the hook (remember to replace it later!), and put a bolt on the door.

REFUSING SEX. Unless there is a genuine and legitimate reason, the refusal of the partner's advances is forbidden in Islam. It is a hurtful rejection. Men and women should realise that sometimes the partner has a very strong urge, which may prevent sleep, and should be kind.

The texts of *Shari'a* affirm that the wife, too, has the *right* to sex.

If either partner is 'not in the mood', or perhaps is in deep sleep when the other partner feels amorous, it is un-Islamic and bad manners to bluntly reject the other. Men, because of the very obvious physical nature of their arousal, often find it hard to understand a woman's needs, which do not show themselves so conspicuously; they should bear in mind that the urge can be just as overwhelming and just as frustrating if not fulfilled.

REWARD FOR SEX. The Prophet (ﷺ) actually spoke of a man's unselfish sexual fulfilment of his wife's needs as a *sadaqa*:

> 'In every declaration of *subhan Allah* there is a *sadaqa*; in every *takbir*, in every *al-hamdu li'Llah*, in every *la ilaha illa'Llah*, in every enjoining of good there is *sadaqa*. Forbidding that which is evil is *sadaqa*. And in a man's sexual intercourse with his wife there is *sadaqa*.' (Muslim)

For more on this see pages 83-106 above.

SAFE PERIOD. Some people try to avoid pregnancy without using contraceptives by only making love during the so-called 'safe-period' - usually the middle days of the menstrual cycle. This is not a reliable method, and has a failure rate of up to 30%. See page 116 above.

SCENT. This is *sunna*, although the wife should obviously not use it carelessly outside the home! But some people find the excessive use of scent by a partner to be irritating, and this should be looked out for.

SENSE OF HUMOUR. A vital ingredient in a marriage. According to a hadith, 'Allah's Messenger was one of the most humorous of people.' (Bazzar, Tabarani.) Remember, it is always kinder to laugh at yourself than at someone else. Also bear in mind that it is against the *sunna* to make people laugh by making something up.

SEX MANUALS. Vast numbers of these are now available in ordinary bookshops. Unfortunately, almost all the recent ones are illustrated, and contain assumptions and practices which are unacceptable in Islam. Anything published before about 1970 is likely to be useful, stressing many of the basic questions of hygiene and morality which Muslims share.

There are dozens of excellent sex manuals in Arabic. Some of these are extremely advanced, far more so, in fact, than most non-Muslim works available in the West. Many great ulema wrote such books, including Ibn Jama'a and Ibn Kamal. Imam al-Suyuti wrote no fewer than eight books on sexual technique! Sadly, these are not yet available in English.

SODOMY. See above under 'Anal Intercourse'.

SORENESS. The 'nappy rash' type can be treated with baby's zinc and castor oil cream, or Drapolene. See also 'Thrush'.

SOUNDPROOFING. Children can find it very distressing to overhear sounds of their parents in bed. Adults, too, will not wish to be overheard by anyone. Try to arrange some kind of soundproofing for your room to ensure privacy - shut the windows, pull the curtains, and perhaps hang a curtain over the door.

SPORT. It is a *sunna* to remain fit, and several types of sport are specifically recommended. They should not, of course, turn into an obsession. If the husband has to play sport every Saturday or

Sunday, the wife should learn to live with this and use the time for things she can do better while he is out of the way. Husbands - remember your wife's good grace, and reward her!

Husbands need to remember that wives do not *always* want to watch sport on TV, and have a right to see some programmes of their choice too. Wives need to know that a real football fanatic cannot possibly be shifted from the 'box' when a particular match is on, and will resist all pressure or temptation. There is no point in a wife trying to prove to herself that he loves her by attempting to seduce him while he is trying to watch the World Cup; he will only get more and more irritated by her. She should not 'bash her head against a brick wall', but make the husband comfortable, see to his needs, and pick up his gratitude afterwards!

TEASING AND MENTAL CRUELTY. This is not permissible. Most women get very hurt by their husband's hankering after beautiful women on TV, videos, or in magazines. Husbands should learn the Islamic virtues of tact and contentment, and realise that a wife is not a model or a film-star, and may have all sorts of physical defects - but she loves you very much, and it is bad-mannered and wrong to hurt her feelings or deliberately make her jealous. Remember that film-stars and models are forever young and willing to please, whereas real human women get older, have aches and pains, get tired, and may not be overcome with enthusiasm for you. Remember that you too are not getting any younger! And remember that you should not be looking at those other women anyway ... (see Sura 24:30-31).

'Beware of envy, for envy devours good works as fire devours wood.' (Hadith in Ibn Maja.)

TEMPTATION. Just because a person gets married, they are not suddenly made blind, or incapable of feeling a sudden urge for someone outside the marriage. It is vital that one deals promptly with the urge, so that the marriage partner is not hurt, the marriage is not weakened, and the possibility of major sin is averted. See page 63 above.

A hadith tells us that the eye can commit *zina*. And as Imam al-Ghazali points out:

'the *zina* of the eye is one of the major faults, and soon leads on to a mortal and obscene sin, which is the *zina* of the flesh. The man who is unable to turn away his eyes will not be able to safeguard himself against unchastity.' (*Disciplining the Soul*)

In the Holy Quran (24:30-1) we read:

'Tell the believing men to lower their gaze and preserve their chastity. That is purer for them. Assuredly, Allah is Aware of what they do. And tell the believing women to lower their gaze and preserve their chastity ...'

And the Prophet (ﷺ) said:

'A gaze is a poisoned arrow from Satan. Whoever abstains from it in fear of Allah shall receive from Him an increase in faith, the sweetness of which he shall feel in his heart.' (Ibn Hanbal)

The Prophet Yahya was once asked: 'How does fornication begin?' and he replied: 'With looking and wishing.'

No-one should ever be too confident about his or her ability to control the sex drive. Al-Fayyad ibn Najih said: 'When a man's penis becomes erect, two-thirds of his reason departs.' It is for this reason that *khalwa* - being alone with a non-*mahram* member of the opposite sex - is not permitted. Often *taqwa* is the only force powerful enough to save human beings from the disaster of adultery - and it is easy to overestimate the degree of one's own piety!

'A leading man of Basra once went into his garden. By chance his eye fell upon the beautiful wife of his gardener. He sent the fellow away on some business and said to the woman: 'Shut the gates!' She replied: 'I have shut them all, except for one which I cannot shut.' 'Which one is that?' he asked, and she replied: 'The gate that is between us and Allah.' On receiving this answer the man repented, and asked for Allah's forgiveness.'
(Ghazali, *Disciplining the Soul*, xxxix.)

THRUSH. A fungal infection of the female sex organs. Canesten HC cream is available from chemists, and will solve the problem very quickly. The husband should also be treated, as it is possible that he has caught it as well, and may be showing flu-like symptoms.

TIMING. It is bad manners to leave your sexual activity until you have gone to bed exhausted. It is a kind of insult, and a marital time-bomb. People's sleep-patterns are important: if a husband comes to bed at midnight, while the wife has dropped off just after the last prayer, midnight may feel early to him and she may be groggy if she is woken from a deep sleep. Tempers are bound to be frayed in the morning.

People are usually either 'owls' (active at night) or 'larks' (active in the early morning). If your partner is the opposite to you, you must sort out an acceptable compromise routine. Be considerate, and compliment your spouse by setting aside proper and suitable times for lovemaking, especially during Ramadan. See page 94 above.

TOLERANCE (*tasamuh*). Remember that husband and wife, however compatible, will always be two different people. Live and let live - do not try to force somebody else to be what they are not; it never works, and only causes resentment. Accept people for what they are and love them 'warts and all'. Be tolerant, forgiving, and understanding, as far as you are able.

> 'O you who believe! Some of your spouses and children can be your foes, so be careful with them. Yet if you pardon and forgive them, Allah will likewise be forgiving and merciful.' (64:14)

> 'Seek reconciliation with those who avoid you, give to those who withhold from you, and forgive those who deal with you un-justly.' (Hadith in Khara'iti)

> 'I was sent only to perfect the noble qualities of character.' (Hadith in Malik, *Muwatta'*)

> 'You will not be able to suffice all people with your wealth; suffice them therefore with a cheerful face and goodness of character.' (Hadith in Hakim, *Mustadrak*)

> 'Whichever man is patient with the bad character of his wife shall be given a reward like unto that which Job shall receive; and whichever woman is patient with the bad character of her hus-band shall be given a reward like that of Asiya the (believing) wife of Pharoah.' (Al-Ghazali)

135

TREADING. A form of massage very common in the Subcontinent, where one partner lies face down and the other 'walks' up and down on them. It is very pleasurable and beneficial, but be careful - the skill has to be learnt. One can usually tread successfully on shoulders, the lower back, buttocks and thighs. Get someone to teach you, or, failing that, buy a massage book. The person doing the treading usually rests on a table, or has a pole (such as a broom handle) to balance with.

UNISEX. The Blessed Prophet had a great respect for natural distinctions. He did not like 'men who try to resemble women, and women who try to resemble men'. (Bukhari.) Be proud of your gender, and ask yourself whether you have the virtues specific to your sex, as exemplified in the lives of the great male and female Companions. There is nothing more pathetic than the sight of 'soft' modern males, who often infuriate their wives through their lack of decisiveness and leadership. Similarly, the decline of femininity has deprived many societies of the most indispensible reservoir of gentleness and beauty. Keep the poles magnetised if you want real attraction to continue between you!

WASHING. Allah has ordained that *ghusl* should be carried out (a) after sexual intercourse (meaning penetration of the penis beyond its head), or whenever an orgasm has occurred (in men and women); (b) after menstruation; (c) after post-childbirth bleeding. (Suras 2:222; 4:43; 5:7.) This involves making a *niyya*, washing off impurities, cleaning the private parts, and then pouring pure water over the entire body and rubbing it at least once. As regards ladies' hair, three handfuls thrown on the head are sufficient; it is not necessary for the plaits to be undone. Warm water can be used; it is preferred to offer two *rak'as* upon completion.

The recorded *sunna* is that if a man wishes to have sex a second time before he has carried out his *ghusl*, he should wash his genitals first. If he had a wet dream, or urinated, he should likewise wash them before having intercourse. There are, however, some traditions from A'isha that suggest that the Prophet (ﷺ) sometimes slept in the state of *janaba* without having touched any water.

136

WEDDINGS. It is *sunna* to hold a feast (*walima*) for a wedding. This is part of the duty to make the marriage public. The Prophet (☻) said: 'Publicise this marriage; celebrate it in the mosques; sound the tambourines to mark it!' (Tirmidhi.)

> Al-Rubayyi bint Muawwidh narrated: 'The Messenger of God (☻) visited me the morning after my marriage was consummated. He sat on my bedding while some servant-girls of ours began to play tambourine and sang eulogies of my ancestors who had died at the battle of Badr. Then one of them said: "And among us is a Prophet who knows what tomorrow brings." But he said to her: "Stop that, but say what you were saying before".' (Bukhari)

> Amir ibn Sa'd said: 'Going in and finding Qaraza ibn Ka'b and Abu Mas'ud al-Ansari at a wedding where girls were singing, I said: "Is this being done in the presence of you two who are companions of God's Messenger, and were present at Badr?" They replied: "Sit down if you wish and listen along with us; or go away if you wish, for we have been given permission for amusement at a wedding."' (Nasa'i)

The actual form of weddings depends a lot on cultural backgrounds, which nowadays are often very un-Islamic in insisting on extravagance and show. The good Muslim practice is always against ostentation or waste in any form, and true Muslim weddings are happy but simple affairs. It often happens that young people have to defer marriage because they cannot afford the parties, and sometimes people demand an enormous *mahr* for the bride. Both practices undermine society and are un-Islamic. It is obviously important for a bride to receive a generous *mahr*, as an insurance policy in case of divorce and to ensure her financial independence. But this is a concession to human frailty. Hadiths recorded by Abu Daud and Tirmidhi show that the Prophet (☻) forbade the giving of excessive dowries.

WET DREAMS (*ihtilam*). These usually happen when people are sexually frustrated, and are a mechanism whereby the body seeks to discharge excess sexual energy or sperm. They can happen to either sex. Both A'isha and Umm Salama asked the Prophet (☻)

about this subject, and were told it was natural. *Ghusl* is of course required afterwards.

WHITE LIES. The Blessed Prophet was realistic. He allowed telling untruths in two circumstances: 'falsehood spoken by a man to his wife in order to reconcile her, and falsehood spoken to set things right between people.'.

12 *A Few Rules for a Happy Marriage*

1   Tell each other you love each other.
2   Never both be angry at the same time.
3   If you have to criticise, do it lovingly.
4   Never bring up old mistakes.
5   Never go to sleep with an argument unsettled.
6   Neglect the whole *dunya* rather than each other.
7   Pray together at least once a day.
8   Remember that behind every successful spouse is an exhausted partner.
9   Remember it takes two to quarrel.
10 When you have done something wrong, admit it.
11 At least once a day, say something kind or complimentary to your partner.
12 Do not go to bed more than ten minutes after your partner.
13 Listen when your partner is speaking.
14 Remember that your spouse is more important than the television/match/video etc.
15 Notice when your partner is wearing something new, or has a new hairdo.
16 Remember anniversaries.
17 Thank your partner for their gift, or effort on your behalf.
18 Last one up, make the bed.
19 Notice when your spouse looks tired, and do something about it.
20 Never run your partner down, or criticise them in public.

Suggestions for Further Reading

The Holy Quran.
Al-Tabrizi, *Mishkat al-Masabih*. Tr. James Robson. Lahore: 1970.

Akhtar, Shabbir. *The Muslim Parent's Handbook*. London:
    Taha, 1993.
Bashier, Zakaria. *Muslim Women in the Midst of Change*.
    Leicester: The Islamic Foundation, 1980.
Bly, Robert. *Iron John. A Book about Men*. Shaftesbury:
    Element Books, 1991.
Buckley, Silma. *Islamic Parenting: The Natural Alternative*.
    Singapore: Muslim Converts Association, 1991.
Chishti, Hakim G.M. *The Traditional Healer*. Wellingborough,
    1988.
Doi, Abdur Rahman. *Women in Shariah*. London: TaHa, 1989.
Faruqi, Lamya'. *Women, Muslim Society and Islam*.
    Indianapolis: American Trust Publications, 1988/1408.
al-Ghazali, Muhammad. *Disciplining the Soul*. Translated by T.J.
    Winter. Cambridge: Islamic Texts Society, 1995.
Khan, G.M. *Personal Hygiene in Islam*. London: Taha.
Khattab, Huda. *The Muslim Woman's Handbook*. London: TaHa
    Publishers, 1993/1413.
Lemu, Aisha B. and Hereen, Fatima. *Women in Islam*.
    Leicester: The Islamic Foundation, 1976/1396.
Lings, Martin. *Muhammad. His life based on the earliest sources*.
    Cambridge: Islamic Texts Society, 1993.
Madani, S.M. *The Family of the Holy Prophet*. Delhi: Adam
    Publishers, n.d.

Further Reading

Musallam, Basim. *Sex and Society in Islam*. Cambridge: Cambridge University Press, 1983.

Rahman, Afzalur. *The Role of Muslim Women in Society*. London: Seerah Foundation, 1986.

Schleifer, Alia. *Motherhood in Islam*. Cambridge: The Islamic Academy, 1986.

Sheikh, N.M. *Woman in Muslim Society*. Karachi: International Islamic Publishers, 1987.

Siddiqui, M.S. *The Blessed Women of Islam*. Lahore: Kazi Publications, 1982.

Thomson, Ahmad. *The Wives of the Prophet Muhammad*. London: Taha, 1993.

Waddy, Charis. *Women in Muslim History*. London: Longmans, 1980.

Many of these books are available by mail-order from The Green Street Bookshop, P.O. Box 842, Bartlow, Cambridge CB1 6PX, England.

Finally...

This elegy was written by Imam Abdallah al-Haddad (d.1132 A.H.) in remembrance of his late wife, the *sayyida* Khadija bint al-sayyid Abdallah bin Umar bin Hussain Faqih.

May Allah water Bashshar with a downpour of mercy
  which rains over it every morning and eve.
There are the meadows of the ones the heart loves,
  and of all who sowed affection for them in their hearts.
May the All-Merciful God greet them with pardon and acceptance,
  And confer upon them excellence, closeness, and all intimacy.
For therein are my loved ones, my family and my lords,
  and our shaikhs who were good to us, and who nurtured us.

And forget not that among the graves at Zinbil,
  Is a grave whose memory will never be erased.
It contains a close friend, righteous, full of blessings,
  - a noble grave it is, a noble place of rest.
I buried in it the one in whom I found my refreshment and my rest,
  after she was gone, I bit into life as though it were dried-out bread.
Hence you find in me nought but grief for the loss of her;
  the voices that console me for her absence are dumb.

So, O Mercy of the All-Merciful, visit her, and rest upon her grave,
  until delight and sweetness of soul are hers,
Send to her my greeting of salaam, and bring her ease,
  a breeze of good-pleasure and nearness both hidden and perceived.

For who may hope for immortality after the loss of Ahmad,
  Prophet of Guidance, whose light put the very sun to shame?